Gildencroft
Let their lives speak

First published in the United Kingdom by Moofix in 2012

Moofix, Rowan House,
28 Queens Road, Hethersett,
Norwich NR9 3DB

ISBN 978-0-9573529-1-9

A CIP Catalogue for this book is available from the British Library

4 2 1 3
2nd Edition

This book can be ordered direct from the publisher, but try your local bookshop first (or the Quaker Meeting House on Upper Goat Lane, Norwich)

moofix

Contents

Introduction

Push open the gate and you exchange tarmac for grass pathways.

A green oasis greets you. You have found a hidden treasure, a sanctuary in a bustling city, a place of peace and quiet. Sit... rest... look around you and let its spirit move. You have come to the Gildencroft and the silence welcomes you.

The Gildencroft is a tranquil acre of land organically managed ; a haven for birds, bees, insects and wildlife. A Place for quiet contemplation and reflection, a simple lunch break, a stroll through the avenue of limes, breathing space in a busy world…

Resting here are remains of thousands of Friends, also known as Quakers or Members of the Religious Society of Friends.

This has been a burial ground since 1670, still in use today and cared for by Norwich Quakers who meet for silent worship at the nearby Meeting House on Upper Goat Lane.

Come and explore and take time to discover more about the lives of the Friends who have made this their home.

This book reveals the lives of friends who are resident at the Gildencroft, used as Norwich Quaker Community's burial ground since 1670. Sue Debbage , a past Warden of Norwich Quaker Meeting with a keen interest in local history, has researched and written an 'alphabet' celebrating their lives and times. Deb Arrowsmith, the present Warden, suggested the idea as a way of bringing the burial ground and the lives therein back 'into' the Meeting. They have also collaborated in devising a travelling exhibition with extracts from the book together with photographs taken through the seasons in the Gildencroft as a way of showing others how to 'enrich the spirit ' alive in their own outdoor spaces. The Gildencroft continues to thrive under the Wardenship of Frances Warns who provided many of the photographs, who organises work parties for its care and upkeep, involves

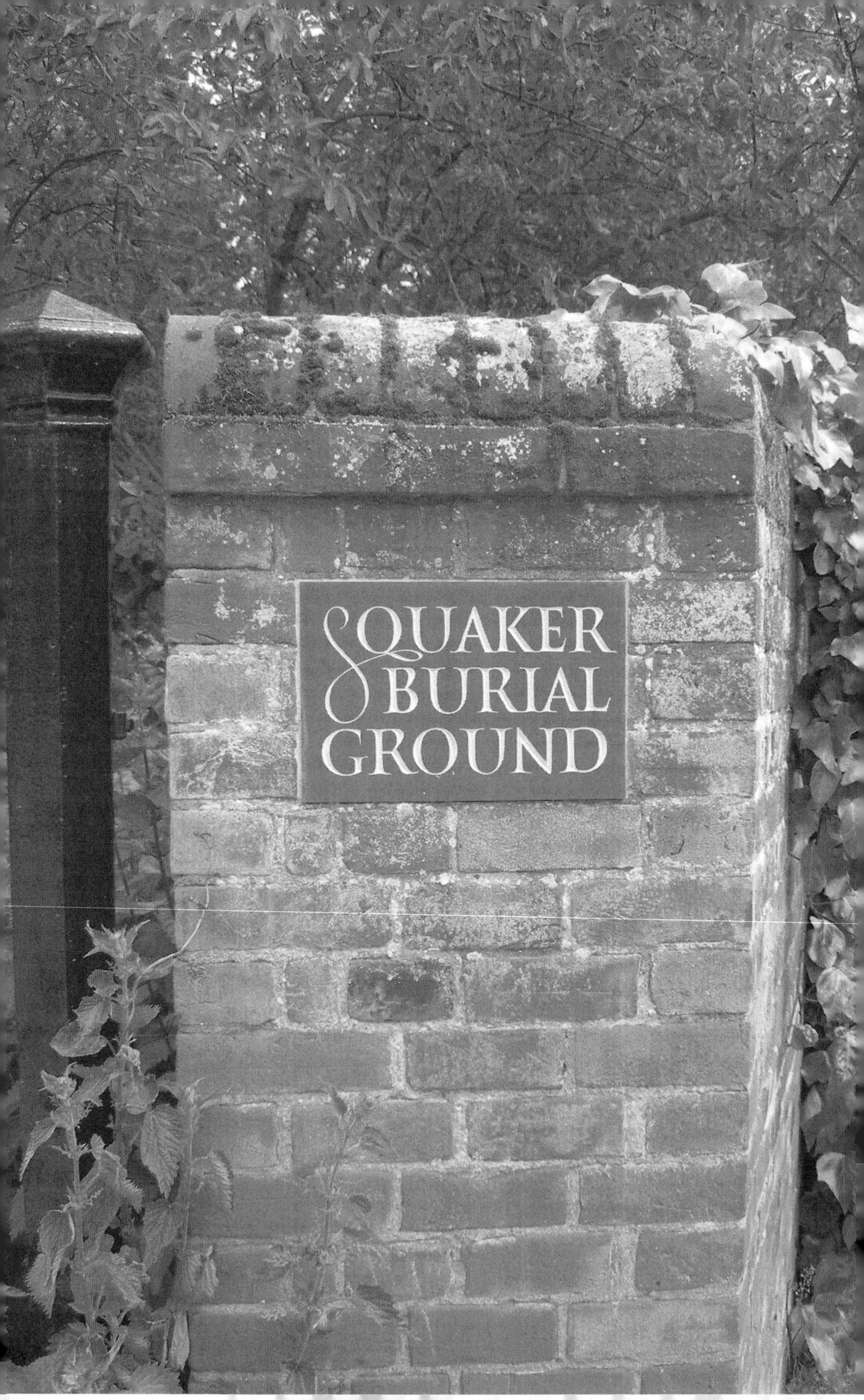
QUAKER
BURIAL
GROUND

craftspeople in creating benches and plaques and who, like many, loves this simple place.

This book and exhibition form part of the work of The Quaker Gardens Project that Deb instigated to raise the profile of the gardens and burial grounds of Quaker Meetings all around the country. These are pieces of land within our care that should, as Quakers say "speak of our condition" They are outdoor, outreach spaces - full of stories from the past but also now imaginatively used and managed as playgrounds, allotments and orchards. Many provide valuable breathing spaces, green oases of calm in busy cities and valuable places of peace and tranquillity.

So, Sit back, read and discover yourself there...

Michael Harvey (the blacksmith who made this bench) and Frances Warns.

Quaker gardens and burial grounds such as the Gildencroft tell stories of our past and the past lives that influenced them. They are also very much in need to be part of our future, especially where spiritual open space, tranquillity and peace are often elusive but so desired.

Quakers hold in common four "testimonies" or ways of living which are Simplicity, Equality, Truth and Peace. Some would add to that a commitment to sustainability in honouring our Earth and its environment. Walking through the Gildencroft; in reality or through the leaves of this book, you will notice the uniformity of the gravestones shapes and inscriptions-simplicity and equality. You will come to learn more of the truth of these characters who chose to remain here as "Friends in residence" and you are sure to meet the deep peace of the place we know as the Gildencroft.

May you carry that peace with you as you go.

As part of the Quaker Garden Project my gratitude goes to James Taylor for his invaluable help in publishing this story, to Sue Debbage whose eyes lit up at the prospect of writing it and to all those who, reading it, come to value our Quaker green and special places.

Deb Arrowsmith 2012.

Note on the 'Let their Lives Speak 'Exhibition

The Exhibition of the Gildencroft which accompanies the book "Let their Lives speak", is available to Meeting Houses on short loan from the Quaker Garden Project. It features 30 A3 size panels all with colour photographs and extracts from the text of "Let their Lives Speak" There are also notes on activities and events that Meetings may organise to help bring their own burial grounds back into the life of the Meeting.

Contact:

QGP
c/o Norwich Meeting
Upper Goat Lane
Norwich
NR2 1EW

or look for details on the website:

www. quakergardensproject.org.uk

A Quick Guide

As the audience who might be interested in this book grew, a very quick guide to the Quakers was deemed necessary: whilst entire books could be dedicated to this topic alone, this is a quick guide:

For more information please visit:

http://www.quaker.org.uk/aboutquakers

There are Quaker meetings all over Britain where more than 20,000 people of all ages and backgrounds worship in stillness to experience the divine directly within themselves, in their relationships with others and with the world around them. Quakerism is a way of life built upon principles of truth, equality, peace and simplicity rather than a written set of beliefs and Quakers have a long-held commitment to putting their faith into direct action in the world.

Quakers do not share a fixed set of beliefs. Our unity is based on shared understanding and a shared practice of worship, not on our beliefs all being the same. There is no need to be in unity with Quakers on every issue in order to be part of our meetings.

There is a great diversity within the Quakers on conceptions of God, and we use different kinds of language to describe religious experience. Some Quakers have a conception of God which is similar to that of orthodox Christians, and would use similar language. Others are happy to use God-centred language, but would conceive of God in very different terms to the traditional Christian trinity. Some describe themselves as agnostics, or humanists, or non-theists and describe their experiences in ways that avoid the use of the word God entirely. Quaker faith is built on experience and Quakers would generally hold that it is the spiritual experience which is central to Quaker worship, and not the use of a particular form of words (whether that be "God" or anything else).[1]

The word **Meeting** may refer to one of several things:

1) the area 'group' of the Quakers (such as the Norwich Meeting or the London Meeting),

2) the 'Meeting for Worship', which is an event held (currently) twice a week for prayer and reflection,

3) the 'Meeting House' which is the physical location of the Meeting (currently Upper Goat Lane)

4) the 'Monthly Meeting' is the administration meeting (which is more of a business meeting) of the Meeting. It is where apointments and accounts are kept and decisions made.

Minute Books: Quaker Meetings have a regular monthly meeting of which the minutes are recorded and kept. The earliest ones were kept in triplicate: one copy for the local Meeting, one copy to be stored in London and the third copy for The Lord himself. These are the primary sources for the information in this book, many of which are now stored at the Norfolk Archive (quoted as N.R.O.).

Overseers are charged with the pastoral well being of the members of the Meeting. **Elders** are charged with the spiritual well being. They are usually appointed by their peers and serve for an agreed number of years (usually three).

Dates: Quakers initially had some difficulty with months and days being named after pagan norse gods. They therefore numbered them; hence the text, where quoting, show (for example) 13th day, first month, year, and First Day Schools being Sunday School.

1 Quoted from Quaker.org.uk

Who's Who

Whilst there are many people interred in the Gildencroft burial ground, throughout this book, and the history of the Norwich Quakers, there are a few names which crop up again and again, either because of their position, because of their actions, or perhaps just because the records made by these people have survived. To help with those unfamiliar with our rich history, a quick 'whos who' of some of the usual suspects. Many of these names are dealt with in detail in their own chapters, but do appear in others.

Arthur Eddington (See "The Eddington Family") was heavily involved in the 1930's and 40's for storing many records to do with the Quaker history at the time. The 'Eddington Papers' refer to his work.

The Gurney Family throughout the 18th and 19th century were very influential both in the Society and in the Textile and Banking industries. Because of their wealth and influence, they had a large part to play in our history. Their bank and textile business records are held in the Norfolk Archive.

Amelia Opie was an author in the Victorian era - she is covered in detail later on. Because of her occupation, there survives a lot of correspondance and information from and about her.

Our Quaker Burial Ground at The Gildencroft in Norwich is the only burial ground still in use within Norwich's mediaeval city walls.

Until 1661 Quakers held Meetings for Worship in private houses. It was very difficult to bury their dead as the graveyards surrounded each parish church and would only receive their own parishioners. The priests could, and did, refuse grave plots to non-conformists although there are records of "... quaker burials in the churchyard of St Clements beside the Fye bridge..." Early Quakers were, by and large, laid to rest wherever a Friend had some land, such as an orchard, that could be used as a burial ground. The land of John Lawrence at Wramplingham was one example.

As the present Warden of the Burial Ground observes "Their [Quakers] first need was land for the dead rather than for the living..."

By the start of the seventeenth century one part of the Gildencroft near St Martins Gate was known as The Folly Ground and had a beer house called The Tabor Folly. The inhabitants of the City gathered here on warm summer evenings to escape their crowded smelly tenements, "... to sport, dance, drink and make merry..."

This began to worry the Authorities and in 1671, the City Bellman (Towncrier) was "...ordered to give notice to the Inhabitants Beyond The Water [North of the River Wensum] that they forbear to spoil the Grass in The Gildencroft by immoderate Campings and Dauncings there....". Camping was an early form of football also known as campball and described as "a cross between rugby and all in wrestling played by large teams" and in the period following The Commonwealth, Puritans banned such sports. Even so, Gildencroft became known for the wildness of its inhabitants. By 1682, The City Marshalls had been ordered to "... apprehend boys and young fellows in The Guyldencroft and Saint Augustines Churchyard on the Lord's Day in Service and Sermon time."

The Quakers chose a parcel of land at the south face of the city wall. It sits at the junction of the present day Baker Street and St Martin at Oak Wall Lane. It is described on some eighteenth century plans of Norwich as 'The Justing or Jousting Acre'. Norwich's knights and Men At Arms once practiced their martial skills such as Tilting At Quatrains (a swivelling target) with lances on horseback and on foot. A small hill known as Tut or Tot Hill (meaning possibly Lookout Hill) once stood to the west of the Jousting Acre somewhere near to the junction. Here, archers practiced their longbow skills that Edward I had decreed was the ONLY sport that might be played on a Sunday.

So, in 1661, Norwich friends bought this parcel of Gildencroft for £72. The land, owned by The Great Hospital, had formerly been used as a tainting ground. Tainting is a process in the early textile industry whereby a piece of cloth was spread out to dry and bleach after being dyed. Special arrangements had to be agreed with the vendors for the use of a roadway wide enough for a four-wheeled hearse to approach and turn round.

In 1669, Quakers built a Meeting House, their second in the city, on one corner of the land. It was originally intended for Friends living "over the water" who sometimes found it difficult to get to Goat Lane if the Wensum was in flood. It was later used mainly for large regional Meetings and special events. In the 19th century it was leased for many years as a Baptist Church with periodic unsuccessful attempts to actually sell the building.

Until the 1720s there were no gravestones in the Burial Ground in keeping with friends testimony to simplicity so about those early interments, Gildencroft's warden says, "...we may know where but not who."

During World War II Gildencroft' s Meeting House was almost completely destroyed by bombing in the Baedeker Raids of April 1842, when the targets were buildings of purely architectural interest. A small building was reconstructed on the plot in the 1950s by George Skipper and his son around the ruins and this is now leased to the Treehouse Children's Day

Centre.

It has been a long time since regular meetings for Worship were held at the Gildencroft, but now and again, for a special event or because Friends just want to do so, there will be a meeting there still. The burial ground has never ceased to be a valued final resting place for Quakers and a much loved place for Friends and others to enjoy as a peaceful haven in a busy world. That being said, it is not unknown for our Meeting to gather at the Gildencroft, ostensibly for a work party to clear undergrowth or prune trees, light a bonfire and engage in a little restrained Dauncing. We have not, as yet, engaged in archery practice, camping or dauncing immoderately.

This narrative has been arranged alphabetically starting with Q. naturally. Quaker Faith and Practice number 27 advises us to:

> *Live adventurously. When choices arise, do you take the way that offers the fullest opportunity for the use of your gifts in the service of God and the community? Let your life speak. When decisions have to be made, are you ready to join with others in seeking clearness, asking for God's guidance and offering counsel to one another?*

There are lots of adventures in our archives, joys and sadness's, rich and poor alike. Did you know that at one time Goat Lane seems to have had a football team that played in a local league? Are our present Meeting Clerks aware that there are at least two weary Clerks that served Norwich Meeting for thirty years?

And did you know that present day gravemakers are currently on the fourth layer.

We hope that by focussing on those Friends who are already interred in this beautiful ground, we will find a clearer understanding of the life of our Quaker Meeting. We hope that we can let all these Gildencroft lives speak.

R

Refugee

If you Google the name of Ishmail Bashaw, you get just one response (other than our own website); that of a single mention of his presence in Scotland in the late 1700s from an address given to a conference only a few years ago on Islamic Studies in Edinburgh. To those of us who have found him, he is an enigma; we are privileged to share a small space in our Burial Ground with him. A brief biography was published by well-wishers in his lifetime in an attempt to secure funds for his subsistence. The author is grateful to Lucy Parker who has lent her copy in the form of an obscure PDF file downloaded from an American University.

The Turkish Refugee:

> *... being a narrative of the life, sufferings, deliverances and conversion of Ishmail Bashaw, a Mahometan Merchant from Constantinople, who was taken prisoner by the Spaniards. And made a wonderful escape to England Where having become a convert to The Christian Faith, he was Publickly Baptized with the Approbation of the Right Reverend The Lord Bishop of Lincoln.*

The booklet was published "...without any other view than to his benefit and that of his family..."

This is a riches to rags story whereby Bashaw and his English family were reduced "...to travelling all round the country to vend my goods and solicit charity..." He and his family became "obliged to fare hardly and still destitute of any bed but one of chaff..."

Bashaw, a self-confessed illiterate, dictated to his amanuensis

> *"I was born in Turkey, in the City of Adrianople, in the year 1735, and was brought up in the Mahometan religion. My father's name was*

Abraham Bashaw, who was a man of considerable property and figure. He carried on an extensive business in silk manufactory, and was besides an officer in the 31st Company of Janizaries belonging to the Grand Signior[1]*. My mother's name was Cotinjah Futma, a woman of good family, whose fortune was twenty thousand pounds. I was the eldest of ten sons and was named Ishmail…"*

When his mother died, as was the custom Ishmail claimed her fortune to be divided between him and his brothers. His father refused this demand. Ishmail physically fought – with a sword – for the inheritance, wounded his father who gave up his claim. The money was legally divided between the brothers with Ishmail keeping 5000L. Ishmail was then only eighteen and married to a bride of twelve. "Such early marriages are not uncommon", he says and the young couple had two children. His wife also had her own fortune greater than that of his mother and Ismail's place as a Janisary, handed on by his father brought in a further two guineas a day. The young Bashaw family therefore lived in some affluence.

His Janissary position involved collecting taxes from Jews and Christians but it was judicial element of the job that "were too much for [his] spirits…". A Janissary was required to conduct executions by flaying the skin of the offender whilst they were still alive - he recounts:

"I could not do it without great difficulty. The anguish of this poor wretch was so extreme that when I had cut off his skin on one side of his neck I purposely cut his throat to put him out of his misery…" Risking his own life, Ishmail claimed to the audience that he had done it accidently by " a flip of the razor".

He vowed never to conduct an execution again, pretended to be ill and resigned the office and took to trade and industry buying a ship sailing between Tunis and Smyrna. As well as its mixed cargo he had on board a large chest of gold. Word of this got about and the ship was attacked by two heavily armed Spanish privateers. A fierce fight ensued until Ishmail had only twenty three men left alive out of fifty and twelve wounded. Hurriedly he gathered an amount of gold from the chest and hid it about his person. The survivors were taken to Carthage where he and his clerk were imprisoned for a year. The two were subsequently forced to work in the Spanish galleons.

Then they were made to labour for stone masons erecting high buildings but as the two men were chained together, climbing the ladders and

1 This equates to an Infantryman in the Turkish Army.

the sheer height at which they were made to work made Ishmail "giddy" and which "exposed [him] to the severe resentment of employers".

The King of Spain ordered that three hundred Turkish slaves should be taken to Madrid; Ishmail and Antonio his clerk were among them. His violent temper answering back an officer resulted in his being branded with a hot iron on the top of his head and a further five years in prison for them both.

He had a fair idea of the country and the route to Portugal. Ishmail, being unable to do it himself, asked Antonio to write to the English Consul at Oporto, John White, asking him to get a message to his younger brother, who had been last heard of in London. At the same time he bribed some of the Spanish prison workers who routinely brought in tobacco and other things to also bring in nitric acid and a small hacksaw which were hidden under a flagstone in their cell. Over the course of three nights he sawed through the bars across the windows "taking care to cover the crevices with dirt" but they could not get the chains off either of their legs. Not without some trepidation, "… some mixture of terror should we be discovered…", the two climbed out of the window on the appointed night;"… my clerk indeed was so terrified of being detected that he was rather averse to the attempt, and at the critical moment began to cry in such a manner that I found it necessary to threaten if he would not be quiet I would run him through…".

Thinking it only safe to travel at night, they hid in an oak tree in a wood some distance from the prison. They were hotly pursued by the authorities coming so close to the escapees that they could be overheard, according to Bashaw's account, saying "If I could find that damned Turk I would run him through the body…". Ishmail earnestly lifted up his heart to God for their protection and prayed that He would blind the pursuers eyes. About ten o clock the next night he and Antonio ventured down from their tree praising a God who had directed them to such a refuge.

They travelled onwards, away from the public roads. On the third night, though exhausted, they were safe in Oporto, Portugal, and asked some persons in the street the way to the house of the English Consul. They got admittance but the Consul had gone to bed…

> *"After eating a morsel of bread, I begged for a pipe of tobacco, but before I had smoaked [sic] it I found myself exceedingly sick. I drank a little wine which threw me into a violent heat. My fellow traveller was worse than myself. A bed was got ready for us and we were glad to betake ourselves to rest. Never was rest so sweet before… [The consul] very kindly addressed me and said 'Get up Ishmail, you shall not be hurt'"*

The consul helped the two men to remove the last of the chains from their legs and bade his servant throw them into the sea. Ishmail fairly quickly recovered but Antonio's mind was uneasy and fearful of what they yet might have to go through in order to get back to their own country.

"Oh Master, I cannot help it: indeed I cannot…".

Ishmail begged him not to distress himself but anything he said was in vain. In about a week, Antonio died.

Ishmail stayed with the consul between two and three years but still felt an earnest longing for Turkey. He would pray every day in the Mahometan manner, in the garden of the Consulate asking God to keep him safe and get him home. At length, The consul discovered that Joseph, Ishmail's brother, had after all gone with the Algerian Ambassador to London. Ishmail resolved to join him and obtained a passage to Dover. In London, Ishmail discovered that his brother had returned to Algiers as secretary to the Ambassador.

Not entirely destitute because of the gold coins he still had secreted about his person he took lodging with a Mr Paget on Tower Hill where he stayed for a year and a half. "I frequented the Exchange and the coffee houses in hopes of meeting with somebody with whom I might return home…" But it must have become known that he carried money because he was robbed at knifepoint in a Whitechapel street. "I was much surprised as well as terrified at this robbery, in a Christian country, having been used to think myself as safe here as at home… From this time I had an abhorrence of London."

He took off for the countryside towards Bristol but found himself no better off there being obliged to lie in the streets. Befriended by a Justice of the Peace who collected money for him, Ishmail was persuaded to return to the capital. Continuously reminded of how he was robbed, he determined again to get away from London. He wanted above all to get back to Turkey. He devised a plan to go to Scotland, there look for a passage to the continent and to Poland and home.

He mistook directions and instead of going towards York he found himself in Ipswich. Here he could get no work so was forced to sleep rough once more and ask for charity. Two gentlemen were particularly kind, Mr Wallis and Mr Spooner and advised him to go to Yarmouth for a passage across the Channel. No boat would take him so he resolved to go to Scotland once more while taking better care to be in the right direction. In Doncaster he was picked up off the streets by a Constable who took him to a lodging house…

> *"An abandoned woman came into my bed and upon finding me not to answer her purpose she lodged a complaint against me, in conse-*

THE TURKISH REFUGEE:

BEING

A NARRATIVE

OF THE

LIFE, SUFFERINGS, DELIVERANCES, AND CONVERSION,

OF

ISHMAEL BASHAW,

A MAHOMETAN MERCHANT, FROM CONSTANTINOPLE, WHO WAS TAKEN PRISONER BY THE SPANIARDS, AND MADE A WONDERFUL ESCAPE TO ENGLAND.

Where, having become a Convert to the Christian Faith,

HE WAS

PUBLICLY BAPTIZED,

WITH

THE APPROBATION OF THE RIGHT REVEREND

The Lord Bishop of Lincoln.

" *Per varios casus, per tot discrimina rerum.*"

VIRGIL.

" *Be not forgetful to entertain strangers.*"

PAUL.

LONDON:

Printed for the BENEFIT of I. BASHAW and his Family, and sold by him:---also,

BY T. CONDER, BUCKLERSBURY; T. KNOTT, LOMBARD-STREET; AND D. TAYLOR, MILE-END.

quence of which I was ill-used and ordered to leave the town... I was so weak I was hardly able to leave the town..."

In Northallerton he met with humane treatment. A Justice of the Peace who was also a Clergyman made a collection for him and paid his carriage fare to Newcastle with a letter of recommendation to the Mayor. His health improved and Ishmail walked on to Morpeth then on via Berwick upon Tweed to Dunbar where a Mr Alexander Watts gave him "great kindnesses" and lodging. The Lord Provost there gave him another recommendation to the Duke of Buccleugh at Dunkieth.

Ishmail stayed a month at Dunkieth where the Duke questioned him often about life in Turkey and, in French, about religions.

Bashaw dictates how the Duke

"took me with him also to the kirk which was the first time that I entered into a place of Christian worship. I was much struck with the singing and the reading of the scriptures both of which were new to me; for in the Turkish Mosque there is no singing nor is any book made use of, the emir pronouncing everything... I expressed surprise at seeing the minister make use of a book and asked what book it was... [The Duke] told me it was the book of God Almighty. I told him that could not be for God Almighty never writes... What the emirs deliver they receive direct from heaven...."

Conversations continued between Ishmail and the Duke about their respective religions and after some time Ishmail began to express his willingness to become a Christian. He was eager to be baptised there and then. The Duke advised patience and to pray to God regarding his sins. Ishmail was impatient and he records that this impatience caused him much distress wanting to be led in the right way to become a true believer. The Duke wrote a letter for Ishmail to take to a minister in Edinburgh with whom he stayed for a month. The desire to be baptised into Christianity did not diminish. This Minister wrote a letter for Ishmail to take to another Duke who lived on the road to Glasgow.

On the road, not six miles from Edinburgh, Ishmail was robbed yet again. He was "abused as a Turk", and stabbed. He put a handkerchief over the wound and went back to Edinburgh "much exhausted..." and told his story to the Lord Provost. The Provost sent for a surgeon and also for the Duke of Buccleugh. The Duchess "...was much affected with [the] situation and shed tears..." They ordered him to an inn to be taken care of where he stayed for six weeks.

Ishmail's narrative then throws us out a surprise. Whilst he had been in Richmond on his way to York he had met a woman, Elizabeth Forms. They had, as he puts it, formed a connection with intent to marry. He arranged that a letter was written on his behalf, for although he was having instruction in the ways of the Christian man he was still illiterate, asking that they consummate the marriage and she accompany him back to Turkey. The Edinburgh minister tried to dissuade him from this on the grounds that British women expect to be treated differently from the wives and concubines in the East. But Ishmail insisted that they were strongly attached and he would remain faithful to her. The couple would be together anyway; better to be legal and decent. Finally the minister consented to conduct the marriage.

The couple began to walk to Glasgow, then Carlisle, then Preston. All the time he records they were met with kindness. They walked towards York and to Hull still looking for a passage to Holland. They were given letters of recommendation to a ship captain and to the English Ambassador in the Hague. With thirty guineas between them they took a coach to Hull, sailed to Amsterdam, continued to Rotterdam and from there to the Hague where they searched for a ship to take them to Turkey.

The captain asked forty guineas for the fares. The Ambassador negotiated for the couple to work some of their passage but the crew had no need of extra hands.

> *"I have seen reason since to adore the good providence of God for this disappointment. For had I returned to my own country I should have been tempted for my own safety to renounce Christianity in which I was as yet but a small proficient and possibly to have returned to my former course of life by which my wife would have been rendered miserable..."*

Elizabeth asserted that she would go with her husband wherever he went. They were advised to return to England, which they did, entering at Harwich and moving on to Ipswich. Elizabeth was by now pregnant and close to her time. It was winter, they had no proper lodging so slept the night in the butchers' shambles. In the morning, having warmed themselves by the blacksmith's forge they obtained a pass to get themselves to Norwich and assistance. They travelled to Scole and presented themselves as required at the Dolphin public house. They were tricked by the landlord saying there was money to be paid. The justices reprimanded the landlord and the couple set off again on foot for Norwich, travelling only a few miles at a time due to Elizabeth's condition.

At the King's Head in St Stephen's Gate they finally found lodgings. Ishmail had learnt to make little articles with wire and began to peddle them around the marketplace. Some Quakers "took particular notice" of them and listened to the account of their travails. A "certain benevolent lady of that sect" made a collection tor Elizabeth and the baby and took a private room for them. A week later, Elizabeth "fell into labour which proved lingering. The Quakers procured a midwife for her, and attended her with great humanity till she was safely brought to bed of a boy...". I have, as yet, found no Overseers Minutes that confirm Ishmail's story here.]

The child was ill and they sought to have him baptised. The clergyman refused to come unless he was paid "....a shilling for himself, sixpence for the clerk and sixpence for the register....". Quakers gave the couple half a crown. Ishmail wanted to be baptised at the same time.....

"Do you think I will baptise a Turk who cannot say the Lord's Prayer?!" The Quakers were as upset at this response as the couple themselves.

Finding themselves in trouble once more on the streets they set out towards Lynn. Their son died at a village along the way and was buried there. Elizabeth was ill in Lynn and they were helped by an Alderman, inviting them to stay and take Sunday lunch after church service. Again Ishmail applied for Christian baptism. Again this was refused on the grounds of the difficulties (presumably with Ishmail's illiteracy) of preparing him for it. After six week he went to Wisbeach for two weeks, then Spalding.

On the Sunday he went to church. The sexton at the door wanted Ishmail to remove his turban which he refused to do. The minister bade the sexton leave him be but took him into the vestry after the service.

"I began to suspect that I had offended the Christians... and that I was going to suffer some punishment..."

The Clergyman and his curate showed great kindness, speaking French and asked what Ishmail thought of Christian worship. Ishmail reported all the times he had sought to be baptised and had been refused. The Clergyman told Ishmail that he must be able to say the Lord's Prayer, the Creed and the Ten Commandments and offered to teach them to him. He continued to make and sell his wire goods for a living and Elizabeth also read to him from the Gospels. In eight months he "...had it all perfectly...". Rev Dinham wrote to the Bishop of Lincoln about Ishmail's request for baptism. The Bishop required Ishmail to shave his beard and remove his Turkish dress... "Now Ishmail," he said. "You look like an Englishman and a Christian..."

The following Sabbath, Dinham baptised Ishmail amid a great crowd and gave him the Christian name of James. The next Sunday, and on subsequent Sundays wherever he was, Ishmail took Holy Communion. They moved from Spalding to Lincoln and went to thank the Bishop for his blessing. The Bishop promised assistance if they got into any more difficulties. Still trying to scrape a living as an itinerant peddler Ishmail was robbed yet again on the way to Gainsborough. The thief took the pocketbook containing his certificate of baptism and then put him before a Justice of the Peace accusing him of lying about his conversion. A Turk could not be a Christian, he said. Ishmail countered that the Church of England prayed constantly for the conversion of infidels so how was it not possible that one such had indeed been converted? They should write to Dinham for confirmation of Ishmail's status. They were kept in Wakefield bridewell all winter, treated like thieves, had their clothes, belongings and tools plundered. Ishmail was particularly upset to lose the Bible that Dinham had given them.

> *"We had wretched accommodation of every kind and I suffered greatly for the want of tobacco… I had now a poor specimen of Christianity which was almost enough to make me question the truth of it…".*

When time came for the couple to appear before the Quarterly sessions they were forced to walk in leg irons to Doncaster, twenty miles away. Ishmail produced all the testimonials he had been given over the years and the magistrate agreed they had been falsely imprisoned. They were given liberty to go wherever they pleased. Ishmail said he would rather not go as they had been robbed, cruelly treated and illegally imprisoned. The magistrate argued that he had had no hand in any of that. Ishmail told him that he was supposed to be a Christian magistrate and he expected justice from him, asserting also that he would die in prison before he would leave without being compensated. Finally the magistrate spoke kindly and gave them half a guinea each, much less than they had lost. However Ishmail accepted the coins and professed forgiveness for the magistrate.

In Black Barnfly they were assisted by Mr and Mrs Ward with money and clothing and a testimonial which would allow Ishmail and Elizabeth to claim more. They moved on to Sheffield where Ishmail became ill with ague and a fever. A merchant who had experience of trade with the Turks also gave relief. Ishmail hoped to get a few tools to carry on his business and so "earn a bit of bread…". Mr Young of Sheffield sent money and wire and Rev Dinham made a collection amongst his parishioners. The couple seemed now well set up in business and resolved to stay where they were, find some security so that they might avoid imprisonment in the future.

In Stamford Ishmail was contracted to make chains for cartridge boxes for export to America. There he was charged with adultery because he had not been a baptised Christian at the time of their marriage. They agreed to be married a second time and were given a legal certificate. They moved on to Northampton in the hope of work in the textile trade. Ishmail was taken ill with a lump on his neck which was treated at the hospital. They were helped by a schoolmaster, Mr Wooley, who had read an account of Ishmail's baptism in the paper. They stayed in Northampton for six months but could get no real work so made a decision to continue on to Daventry. There the two Mr Checkleys were "particularly kind" and made a collection. They also took Ishmail to the Dissenting[2] academy who also gave support. The couple took a house and by degrees got it furnished. They became established enough to fix a board above their door.

He continued the itinerant life selling wire goods and dyed cloth door to door, while Elizabeth bought glass vials for local apothecaries. He continued to attend church on prayer days and also visited dissenting meetings in the evenings. They report being happier there until "... a fresh storm gathered."

Strictly speaking as he had not served an apprenticeship in Daventry he was not free to trade there unless he bought that freedom. The charge would be five pounds plus a fee to the parish officers. They did not have that money so the bellman [towncrier] went round the town demanding that no one do business with the Bashaws. Although a London wellwisher offered to pay the fee it was decided to move on towards Kettering especially as they now had another child.

In Kettering they met up with some Dissenters, staying briefly and went back to Lincolnshire. He was robbed of a toasting fork again at Newark and faced "disagreeable circumstance" at Grantham. His wife was treated with abuse by two men "...as if she had been a common prostitute...". Reverend Dilham was one of the Magistrates there and fined the men fifty shillings which he ordered to be paid to the family. They travelled on again through Stamford and Spalding, gratefully receiving charity of many friends. Another child was due and many kindnesses were accepted during Elizabeth's confinement. Once she was strong enough the family travelled on to Wisbeach where they took a house and found business in dying textiles. Ishmail attended Lynn markets while Elizabeth continued the business in Wisbeach. "During this period a disagreeable thing happened..."

Being now used to the services of the Church of England and taking Holy Communion he was in church one Sunday. Two boys fought during the service and Ishmail intervened. One of the boys swore at him so Ishmail retaliated with his stick. The parson severely reprimanded him un-

2 Disenters were early english protestants who seperated from the Church of England

willing to listen to the real truth of the matter.

> *"... Such conduct as this excited in my mind such a prejudice that from that time I determined never to hear him again and went among the Dissenters by whose preaching I found myself better instructed in the knowledge of the Gospel..."*

He became acquainted with a local Alderman who became dangerously ill, asking for Ishmail to go to his bedside. Many conversations about religion ensued. The Alderman promised that he would set the family up in business again to the sum of a hundred pounds when he recovered. He was advised to go to Bath for The Cure and arranged for some friends to continue kindnesses to the family. The Alderman died in Bath and actually only left ten pounds. Other friends donated clothing and further amounts of money.

The business continued in Wisbeach and Ishmail began working Norwich markets. He attended Meetings for Worship and was advised to settle in the city. At Reverend Newton's house he was introduced to a Mr Clark who was a stuff weaver[3]. He brought his wife and family over while some gentlemen rented a house for them and assisted in furnishing it. He traded in wire ware and tin ware and did well for seven years. He began to travel about once more selling his goods. Elizabeth was expecting another child and was helped by a Scots Society allowing her three shillings a week.

Ishmail, now forty five years old, was anxious to settle once more and become a member of some Christian church. Friends in Bury collected money to help with a permanent job. A shoemaker was willing to teach him the trade but it was decided Ishmail was too old to start learning. Others suggested he learn woolcombing. Ishmail consulted friends in Norwich and finally decided to make the move to Bury. The other apprentices took against him and the Woolcomber began to find fault with his work. Ishmail begged for more time to learn as his landlord was already coming to him for the rent. The original agreement had been that the Master was responsible for his accommodation. The landlord considered Ishmail had been ill used and behaved kindly towards the family. Ishmail asked local magistrates for his premium back without success. Instead they gave him a small horse and cart and half a guinea to help with his removal. The family now had two live children and another was due.

They arrived at Nayland where this child was born though it died within six weeks in a village close to Ipswich. In Ipswich their fifth child was

3 Norwich Stuff is a local cloth; Gurney and Bland, after their purchase of Stannards exported much of this cloth to Europe.

born, baptised by the sympathetic Reverend Edwards but died soon afterwards. They visited Framlingham and Woodbridge but at length returned to Norwich where as well as selling his tin ware he found dying work with a Mr Moor. The dyer's business failed though he gave Ishmail an honourable written testimonial. Still in need of work he travelled to Beccles beginning the trade of dying and dressing hats. Life was good for the first year and Elizabeth gave birth to their sixth child.

Ishmail journeyed with his donkey loaded with his wares and books to Cambridge and Newmarket. He was beaten and robbed along the road then dammed for being a Turk. He went to Stourbridge fair but had very little left to sell. Again he was helped by the local vicar.

> *"I got a person to inform my wife of my fresh misfortunes who upon reading the letter, shed tears. My eldest girl who was about six and a half years old (an intelligent and affectionate child) observing her mother weep, inquired the cause... At which the poor child was deeply affected expressing her earnest wish to have me return... At this time she was very ill of a consumption brought on by a cold after the measles and did not live to enjoy the satisfaction of my safe arrival... While I was on this unfortunate journey my other two children were ill also, one with the evil the other with a worm fever and that they were all dead and buried before I got back..."*

Three children died in three days. Elizabeth, told by the Parish Officers that there was no reason for her to stay, was sent away. Ishmail, upon hearing of this compound tragedy made all haste to get home. "I found her so ill, partly through great fatigue she being but weakly, partly through poverty but principally through grief, that there was little hope of her life." Church communities prayed for her recovery. Ishmail "felt resigned to the will of God and soon had cause for devout thanksgiving on account of [Elizabeth's] recovery...". However, the Parish demanded twenty five shillings for the burial of his children. Ishmail and Elizabeth sold up and left.

They settled briefly at Walpole, then Framlingham again where they met with several friends. Ishmail remembers the Reverend Mr Toms with particular respect and gratitude. Elizabeth gave birth to their tenth child (which is the only one at this time living). In 1787 the family determined upon returning to London with recommendations from friends in the country, getting such assistance as might enable them to become settled and find honest labour.

What a circumambulation! It is at this point that the published narrative ends and the booklet is produced for sale to help Ishmail on his way.

It may well have worked: It appears that from this point life began to get easier, more prosperous. We know Ishmail is buried in the Gildencroft but not Elizabeth nor their remaining child. We know he came back to Norwich as a relatively successful merchant and lived contentedly another decade or more in Norwich but not whether Elizabeth was with him. Our burial records do not show an Elizabeth interred here that we can match positively. It may be possible to examine the records of the Diocese of Lincoln to find the certificate of their marriage which would show her maiden name. If the child married then it is conceivable that if she returned with her father or indeed both parents then she may be buried under her married name. We just do not know. Ishmail Bashaw remains an enigma.

Ishmail Bashaw. Buried in the Gildencroft 10th June 1815 aged 80.

S

The Adult and First Day School Movement

G. Currie Martin records that the first Adult School came out of a Methodist New Connection Church in Nottingham around the turn of the nineteenth century by William Singleton and

> *"one of his helpers the Quaker Samuel Fox, a grocer in the city and a man looked up to by everyone for his probity and conscientious character"*

The school leaders were mainly recruited from the women assistants of his own shop, closing earlier on Saturday evening than his neighbours in order that everyone might be in the School by seven o'clock on the Sunday morning. When the school, which lasted two hours, was over he invited the teachers to breakfast. Martin supposes that the studies were "... the elements of reading and bible instruction".

About 1830 a library and savings fund had been added, and from eight to nine on three mornings Fox held an arithmetic class for students who wanted to make further progress. This Adult and First Day School Movement spread widely. When the lease of the Gildencroft Meeting House to the Baptists in Norwich ended, the decision was taken to encourage the setting up of classes around the Meeting.

> *The following report has been brought in by the Committee appointed in 10mo 1892 to make such alterations in the Gildencroft Meeting House as were needed to adapt it for a branch Adult School provided the money required for the purpose could be obtained. The report is very satisfactory to this Meeting and thankfulness has been expressed that the appeal for funds was liberally responded to, which with the success that has attended the opening for school and other purpos-*

es cannot but be regarded as evidence that the effort which has been made to utilise the building for the good of the population by which it is surrounded is with the gracious approval of the Lord of the Harvest whose continued blessing we earnestly desire may be abundantly experienced in the future:- Reports

We have pleasure in reporting the completion of the work in connection with the alteration of the Gildencroft Meeting House. We thankfully acknowledge the liberality of the friends who so kindly enabled us to carry out the alterations; of Brightwen Binyon who very materially assisted us with advice and drew out a plan which though not entirely acted upon gave valuable suggestions:- also of J.G. and F.W Skipper the architects in charging four instead of 5 percent.

Our first intention was to lay out about £400 which we thought would render the building useable but after serious consideration we decided to spend a larger sum at once to make it really convenient for all purposes. The galleries and the part underneath have been levelled and made into classrooms divided by curtains, the bottom portion being divided from the centre by two doors and sash shutters on each side and the upper galleries by curtains. An additional entrance has been made, also two new windows and cloak room, boiler room and c have been built – the whole heated with hot water. 272 feet of tables with trestles have been provided and the fixed inconvenient forms made suitable for all purposes, also various outside alterations including a new shed for burial ground materials.

These and other alterations involved an expenditure (including £24.7.2d for Bibles and Hymn books) of £863.17.8 1/2d which is balanced by the donations.

The blessing which has so far rested on the work there satisfies us that the reopening was the right step. The school commenced on Oct 15th; the average attendance for the first two months was 172 and 134 new men attended regularly and became registered scholars. The mothers Meeting commenced on Jan 2nd has had an attendance of 60 or over each time they have met. We trust the way will open for other work shortly.

The expense of printing and postage in connection with raising the needed funds was £4.0.4d.......[list of promised annual subscriptions from Qs]....These will not enable the school to pay the full rent and for gas, coal etc. We therefore suggest that for the present all expenses shall be paid by the Yearly Charge at Goat Lane and that the school pay annually to that a/c not less than the amount of the special subscriptions received.

Signed on behalf of the committee John Sayer.

Norwich Monthly Meeting 2nd Month 1894.[1]

A Bible Class is held once in two weeks for members and attenders, and another similar class once a week for men only, principally those who do not attend our meetings. Also a Meeting for Religious Fellowship is held monthly for the edification of those connected with the Meetings and Schools...."

Norwich Monthly Meeting Elders and Overseers 3rd October 1872[2]

From this modest beginning grew a register of as many as 600 men at the School's peak at Goat Lane. Womens' schools were started, as were classes for children and young people. Classes were for

... lads and lasses between approximately 13 and 17 years... to help avoid a crude determinism and to become Captains of their Souls... Junior sections designed to attract the older boys and youths under

1 N.R.O. SF64.

2 N.R.O. SF86

the age of 17 or thereabouts, who, esteeming themselves too old for the ordinary Sunday School, [were] so often left to shift for themselves, exposed to temptations of all kinds before their characters [had] the strength to resist them...[3]

For there is plenty going on in the week... plenty for everyone to lend a hand to, or a voice, above all a heart... because the School depends so much on each of its members doing her part and giving her thought and care to it, it is so helpful to us...

The classes popularity grew and secular facilities increased. The Early Attendance Fund was introduced. Punctual students had a proportion of their subscription saved for them soon adding up to "... a nest egg of no little value for the purchases of useful and durable articles [often boots and coats] at a time of year when most needed...". Provident Societies formed and were much relied upon in sickness and bereavement. For weekly subscriptions of 3d, payment of 5/- for thirteen weeks followed by 2/6d for thirteen weeks was made. £6 was paid out after an adult's death but only £1 10/- for a child. Voluntary Sick Boxes stood in most classrooms to collect grants. Savings Funds deposits gained 5% interest; upon reaching £20 the interest was lower. By 1889, 96 depositors were in receipt of 4% interest showing that they at least had saved more than the £20.

There were 560 books in the School library. On payment of 2d a week borrowings could be made from the catalogue.

From 1870 onwards many who attended the Adult Schools, though naturally drawn to the religion of their teachers, could not adjust to the silence or haphazard ministry of the Quaker Meeting for Worship. To meet their needs, Eddington widened his evangelical ministry, holding gatherings in public places, engaging speakers and gospellers to visit at the Gildencroft. Services misnamed Mission Meetings were established with prepared addresses and hymn singing. The Adult Schools Movement produced a hymnbook for these Meetings "with sufficient variety... adapted to the many occasions which occur for thanksgiving...".

The scope of spiritual provision widened with Bible meetings and Mothers' Meetings. There was opposition in certain quarters on the grounds that teaching people to read on the Sabbath increased secularisation and teaching writing to the poor might prove a big incentive to forgery. Meals were served before classes began on First Day mornings at tables set with specially commissioned crested china. Financial records declare payment of a final invoice for tableware sufficient for 700 sittings. Whilst this was

3 N.R.O. SF63

a social or economic necessity for some students, Eddington maintained it was a bonding time, an expression of belonging. It nevertheless brought suggestions of Eucharistic leanings.

Fundraising became the norm from cooperative and innovative new members. Occasions such as this sale of work at the Gildencroft Meeting House "… met with the success it deserved, many having worked long and patiently for this end… A brisk trade followed… and as a result a net profit of £50.10/8 1/2d was declared… Much interest was attached to Mr Armstrong's collection of curiosities illustrative of Bible Times which included a model of the Tabernacle, Herod's Temple etc…". [Annual report of Friends First day Schools. 1895.]s

Individual Friends reviewed their own finances forming Coal Clubs, Goose Clubs and Ambulance Classes.

> *To most of these members the school is one of the main interests in life. Men and women again and again say that it has blessed them at home and at work, in head and heart, in health and wealth….*
>
> Pamphlet : Adult Schools 1894. W.C. Braithwaite

There were outings for the children:

"... conveyed to Whitlingham in brakes and on their arrival a bountiful tea was served, various sports followed making up a successful outing..."

Annual report, Norwich Adult School 1889.

There were days out for the adults. Visits to Leicester hosiery factories led to exchange visits no doubt looking at each other's workplaces and practices.

In the schools was the way to give both Quakers and the general population a facility from which it might all benefit, thus encouraging students to come into Membership as will be shown in the life of Henry Rudd Douglas and of Hamilton and Eliza Manthorpe.

Henry Rudd Douglas was a twenty-year-old carpenter at this time.

Minute 5. An application for membership having been received from Henry Rudd Douglas, John Sayer and Henry Brown are appointed to visit him and report.

Norwich Monthly Meeting, 2nd Month 1892[4]

Minute 2. The following is brought in by the friends appointed to visit Henry Rudd Douglas viz. we have had a satisfactory interview with Henry R. Douglas. He was for some years in the Junior School before he was old enough to enter the Men's School and it was during this time that he yielded to the visitations of Divine Grace and gave his heart to the Lord. He has had the subject of applying for membership on his mind for about two years and has made himself acquainted with the Christian views of Friends which he is convinced are scriptural. We recommend that his application be acceded to. John Sayer. Henry Brown.

The recommendation is acceded to and Henry Rudd Douglas is hereby received into membership with our religious society. John Sayer is requested to inform him thereof.

Norwich Monthly Meeting, 3rd Month 1892

Birth notes are brought in ... for a son of Henry R Douglas and Mary, his wife, who was born on the 1st of 1mo at 106 Gladstone St, Norwich, and was named Wilfrid Henry – the birth was reistered at the West Wymer district on the 8th inst.

Norwich Monthly Meeting, 1st Month 1898

---

4 N.R.O. SF64

The Tallowin Family

Several years back, when I was still warden at Goat Lane, two sisters arrived looking for their ancestors.

"They might have been Quakers?" I asked.

"Possibly…."

"How far back?"

"Not sure…."

They were teaching themselves how to use internet ancestry sites now they were retired, and my experience with ancestry websites is that one ends up with a long list of names that may or may not be related to you or each other. One sister held out a whole wedge of A4 sheets of closely printed names. She also clutched one or two quotes from secondary sources; nothing wrong with that, we have used some of what must strictly be classified as secondary sources here thanks to Arthur Eddington [qv] but she had not noted where her sources had come from. One difference between us was that I knew what my original sources were and, most conveniently, where they were. I sat the two ladies down with Christian Barclay and Jane Nolan's index of the catalogue of our archive held at the Norfolk Record Office - at the time nothing was available on line from the N.R.O.

"We found a Stephen Tallowen or Tallowin who got into a bit of a scuffle at Hingham." explained the first.

"Or it might have been Kings Lynn.." corrected the second.

"When?" I asked.

"Oh, a while back…."

After much paper shuffling they found me the quote they had laboriously copied from the book at The Family History Society up the road.

"Did the pamphlet say where it had got its information from?"

They hadn't written that down, but if the quote was right we were talking way back to the start of Quakerism, 1669. If the incident happened then that hotheaded Tallowen either travelled up with, or was persuaded by, Symonds or Hubberthorne. He had been arrested preaching Fox's gospel, disrupting evensong in some steeplehouse or other and had been brought to the attention of the Justices of the Peace.

More than six years ago, maybe even eight, I had researched a piece on 25 The Walk, Samuel Robbin's Gift and the Elizabeth Langwade Gift [qv], following the Meeting's sponsorship of apprentices and Tallowin had come up. As it is not a common name; I remembered it. The three of us put together some entries they had known about and some that were new and the sisters went away happy as sandgirls.

Then, two weeks ago, I took myself down to the Record Office to pull out some old Minute Books with Tallowen/in as one of the names on my list to look for. Examination of the Burials map had revealed a whole row of seventeen family burials in the Gildencroft. Who should I find had signed in at N.R.O. immediately ahead of me? The same sisters sat with our index and catalogue open on the table in front of them. There must be a Greater Spirit guiding us all in our endeavours, we laughed. The women's wedge of papers was even thicker now because they had discovered they themselves were definitely descended from a Stephen Tallowin who had married a Mary. There were, however, more than two and a half centuries of Tallowens, Tallowins and Tallins, even one Talling, many, many of whom were Stephen or Steven and many of them had married a Mary. So in two years or more they weren't that much further forward. They needed a methodology lesson and I could give them one. I could also use what family information they were willing to share.

"Sounds good to me." said the first.

"Sensible." agreed the other.

We made a date to meet back at Goat Lane as they don't like a lot of talking in the Search Room at the Record Office. We planned to get the Gildencroft map out again, the Burials Index, the Register and perhaps have another scurry through the Eddington Works. We knew that at least one of the Tallowen[in] apprentices must have completed his indentures because their family were still Freemen of the City of Norwich in 2012. That privilege is handed down the generations. They could probably find details of the original holder of Freedom of the City from City Annals; these have been ably collated by Norfolk Record Society in one of their annual red leather bound volumes but we all secretly wanted to see if the graves in the Gildencroft could tell us. The sisters could see how the clues could begin to come together. They began to realise they could find out which of the family rumours might or might not be true. In the Burials register we found that some infants' births had been entered twice; it appears that both parents, particularly a Stephen and Mary Tallowin, separately told the overseer responsible for keeping the birth notes each time. Stephen consistently gave both parents' names while Mary only gave Stephen's name. The copyist, someone paid to do the writing and not a member of the Meeting, simply copied down what he was given in six-monthly chunks. Might these be their Stephen and Mary we hoped? Their particular ancestral Tallowen! We all began to thoroughly enjoy ourselves. They stayed to Wednesday lunch, met and talked to more Quakers. Call it outreach.

Stephen Tallowin and Benjamin Tallowin c 1750s

Stephen desires of this Meeting that his son Benjamin Tallowin may be bound Apprentice to Cornelius Herrington, Woolcomber........

Norwich Monthly Meeting 9th mo 1751[1]

It does not appear to this Meeting Cornelius Herrington is a proper Master to bind an Apprentice to by order and at the expence[sic] of this Meeting

Norwich Monthly Meeting 10th mo 1751

Quakers had two trust funds that had been endowed for this purpose and the Master, if not a Quaker himself, had to be above reproach just as much as the prospective apprentice. Herrington, although willing to take the student and probably having a gentleman's agreement with Stephen for his son, was not deemed by Trustees to be a suitable recipient of Friends' funds. There is no record of the Meeting binding Benjamin with any other Master nor any mention of the Tallowins funding themselves with Herrington.

"There's a story in the family that one of them might have been thrown out? Disowned?" offered the sisters. "What does that mean?"

We found several examples of Disunity of Tallowens within the Minute Books, such as Samuel Tallowin in the 1750's.

Samuel, probably a lastmaker from our minutes and the sisters' notes had two apprentices, Benjamin and Isaac Bateman. Elders of the Quaker Meeting:

...from time to time visited and tenderly advised him to desist from many things that were reproachful in his conduct and contrary to the Principles of Truth professed by us....not taking proper care of his family....

---

1 All references this chapter are from N.R.O. SF 55, 56 and 57

He was at the point of insolvency having been

...frequenting Publick houses and other neglects of his Business... and failed in the payment of his just debts... Friends were at pains *....to endeavour that the two apprentices he has now may be afforded such assistance in the mean time as to them shall appear needful...*

Norwich Monthly Meeting 9th mo 1759

Benjamin and Isaac Bateman both apprentices to Samuel Tallowin being at present wholly unemployed and their master incapable to continue them...[Friends] are desired to take the needful care to procure them a legal discharge and to endeavour when discharged to procure them proper places to be put out to...

Norwich Monthly Meeting 9th mo 1759

The Meeting called Samuel to account.:

He said he had nothing to alledge in excuse of his conduct or why a Testimony of Denial should not go forth from this Meeting...Saml. Tallowin's Apprentices are continued under the care of the Friends appointed..."

Samuel lost his membership of the Society:

...for the Clearing of Truth and Friends from the Scandal brought upon them by the said Samuel Tallowin...They can have no fellowship with him or look upon him as in any wise belonging thereunto until it shall appear that by a sincere repentance and Amendment of Conduct, he shall wipe off the reproach he has occasioned by his disorderly walking...

The meeting Trustees made sure that Tallowin's apprentices were not disadvantaged:

Benjamin Bateman is gone to our Friend William Roper, last maker in London, on trial; and ...the other apprentice Isaac Bateman is taken home by his Friends in the Country. It is desired that the said Friends get both their Indentures legally discharged...

Norwich Monthly Meeting 12nd mo 1759

Benjamin Tallowin c1764

Quakers then would only recognise a marriage where both parties were in membership and where the marriage had been in The Manner of Friends. The couple were otherwise considered to be living in sin.

We can have no unity with such marriages nor can we receive the Collections of any so offending or if fall into want relieve them…[They] cannot but be sorrowfully affected...

Norwich Monthly Meeting 2nd mo 1748

Friends found:

…great difficulty [in dealing] with such that marry by the Priest, after Marriage; and which hitherto have been much neglected…[and]… advertise all such that so marry the Consequences thereof…

Norwich Monthly Meeting 2nd mo 1755

…BENJAMIN TALLOWIN son of Stephen Tallowin deceased has been lately married by a Priest. Friend John Gurney with elders are desirous to meet them on behalf of this Meeting and to enquire what they can allege why the Discipline of the Society should not be extended towards them on that occasion…

Norwich Monthly Meeting 12mo 1764

Is this the same Benjamin Tallowin for whom the Meeting refused to pay an Indenture Fee? We believe so. Benjamin also lost his membership of the Society.

Stephen Tallowin Junior 1777 and Benjamin Tallowin 1780.

Stephen (at this time listed as 'absenting himself from Meetings and other inconsistent conduct') is mentioned:

…whose conduct has been highly reproachful to our holy Profession… has inlisted himself for a soldier…

It appears that a younger brother followed him:

…Benjamin Tallowin acknowledged that he has entered a Substitute in the Militia…this Meeting therefore finds itself under the ne-

cessity to declare our Disunity with such conduct…we much desire he may be brought to a due sense of his Outgoing…

Norwich Monthly Meeting 3rd mo 1780

Both young men lost their membership. Quakers' Testimony for Peace and against the Bearing of Arms was of primary concern. But, to Stephen and Benjamin, if there was no employment in the City wouldn't the army life, the promise of travelling and adventure, have seemed a better way forward? It is to be hoped that they kept safe and well, the wars with France were dangerously close.

Samuel Tallowin 1786

It seems that this Samuel had not been coming to Worship.

… On account of his having in great measure declined the Attendance of our religious Meetings notwithstanding the Labours of Love that had been extended towards him by divers Friends… [Elders]… endeavoured to convince him of the great Inconsistency of his Conduct which he did not attempt to justify… [nor]… did give them any Expectation of a satisfactory Alteration…

Norwich Monthly Meeting 10mo 1786

Samuel also lost his membership of the Society.

…Appearing that he continues to absent himself… and manifest a disregard to the Admonitions of Friends… It is our sense and judgement that he is gone from us and we can therefore do no less that declare our Disunity with the said SAMUEL TALLOWIN.

Norwich Monthly Meeting 1st mo 1787

Rebecca Tallowin 1793

… [Rebecca had] for a considerable time absented herself from Meetings and repeated endeavours have been used to visit her but without effect…

Monthly Meeting of Women Friends 6th mo 1793

… She received us in a friendly manner and acknowledged that the Visit and the advice which was imparted manifested the regard and kindness of Friends. She informed us that she had nor join'd herself

with any other religious Society. Nevertheless there did not appear any disposition to renew a closer union with our own...

Norwich Monthly Meeting 7th mo 1793

... Appearing that the labours of Love which have been extended to her have not prevail'd on her mind... She still continuing in the same conduct of remissness therein... Under a painful sense of such great Impropriety..."

Norwich Monthly Meeting 11th mo 1793

Rebecca forfeited her membership.

None of these members of the Tallowin family are buried in the Gildencroft by virtue of them leaving the Society.

There is another Rebecca Tallowin who actually is in the Gildencroft having died on 30th September 1858. Her death certificate is catalogued SF428/1 and her burial note is SF390/8 but, as yet, there is nothing about her from the Minutes Books that we can add to the family narrative. The three of us could still see that whole enticing line of graves with the family name bisecting the Burials Map. We needed to look further. No more Ancestry sites. One sister believed "there might have been a teacher?"

Thomas Tallowin 1748-1825

Quakers were consistently at pains to see their children had a good education. Thomas Tallowin was a teacher though not in the manner we would understand today. There are many minutes recording that the Meeting paid for young Friends to "... be put to school..." with him.

... Ordered that James Blagbourne, son of James Blagbourne, be put to school to Thomas Tallowin, at the expense of this Meeting, one Year whole days or two years half days, to learn to write...

Norwich Monthly Meeting 2nd mo 1772

... This Meeting directs that Lucy Neale be put to school with Thomas Tallowin to learn to write...

Norwich Monthly Meeting 3rd mo 1773

Edmond the Son of the Widow Golder is ordered to be put to School with Thomas Tallowin... and also Elizabeth the daughter of the Wid-

ow Golding is ordered to be put to writing... for one year at the expense of this Meeting...

Norwich Monthly Meeting 4th mo 1774

The account rendered at the end of that year was £2:3/2d for Edmond while Elizabeth's was £2: 3/10d. What had cost Elizabeth an extra eight pence? Frederic Golder was already a student with Tallowin.

31st 3rd mo 1775. Minutes list a bill from Tallowin for two years of teaching at a cost to the Meeting of £4: 9/11d. Ann Standin, daughter of Eli Standin became a new student according to the same minute. The pattern was well established.

Thomas saw out the whole of his life with Norwich Quakers and is buried in the Gildencroft. The sisters claim that at some point in his life, Thomas "did a survey " and produced the first map of the Gildencroft burials. I have not yet found a minute to confirm this but they have been correct about so much else.

There is also a minuted record of a Mehetabel Tallowin nee Pocklington who probably was also a teacher and wife of a Joseph Tallowin. She later took in girls from the Meeting and taught them sewing. For instance, Susanna Ward, Anna Golder, Mary Standin and Ann Seaman are all recorded as pupils for one year with the Meeting paying their premiums. [N.R.O. SF56. Minute dated 27th 2nd mo 1778.] Mehetebel, as a widow, fell on hard times and was herself helped financially at three shillings a week by the Meeting until her death in 1808.

Samuel Tallowin, Stephen Tallowin and Benjamin Tallowin c 1770s

Henry Gurney having proposed to place Samuel Tallowin son of Stephen Tallowin in a Way to be instructed to Weave; and no proper Friend in that Business being found to take him Apprentice...

Norwich Monthly Meeting 2nd mo 1770

Gurney had to look outside the Society for a placement.

Henry Gurney brought to this Meeting the Indenture of Samuel Tallowin, bound Apprentice to John Mann of Mary's parish in this City, Worstead Weaver and the Expence thereof being £7:15/2d... out of the proceeds of the Market Estate and the Indenture lodged...

Norwich Monthly Meeting 6th mo 1770

The present Tallowin family can consult the City Freeman records to discover whether Samuel completed his apprenticeship so becoming Master then Freeman. If he did, then his father, Stephen, might just be the ancestor the sisters believe they are descended from. Stephen had more than one son;

> *Ordered that Benjamin Tallowin the son of Stephen Tallowin be bound apprentice at the expence of this Meeting to James Barney of Mary's Parish in this City, Worstead Weaver for the term of seven years...*

Norwich Monthly Meeting 10th mo 1771

Might Benjamin complete the ancestral line from the sisters?

The Tallowin sisters completed the story. "It was hard times." Benjamin Tallowin died in 1831, "29th March", aged 76. By now, the Norfolk textile trade was in decline due to mechanisation and the location of great factory complexes in northern industrial towns. There was little call for weavers of Benjamin's calibre so he had been forced to support himself by selling milk. He apparently collapsed "... whilst walking on Swan Lane [and] was seized with an attack of apoplexy..." The verdict of the Inquest held at the Swan in St Andrews was "Visitation of God." [N.R.O. Coroners Inquest 1660-1835]

These are some of the confirmed Tallowin family that we have [between the three of us] found so far. The sisters have many years of research yet to do.

We have yet to find the original Tallowin involved in the Hingham fracas that seems to have started the family's connection with Quakers. But.... at the last moment a dear Ffriend presented us with the tantalising reference to a Grace Tallwyn of Morley who was married to a James Hillary at Great Ellingham on 7th of 11th month 1673/4. [Because of the change in the calendar this means that the wedding took place in the January rather than the November.] The villages are close enough to where the Tallowen sisters believe the fracas took place and the dates are close enough to suggest perhaps, just perhaps Grace was the daughter of the Stephen Tallowen we have been searching for. Who knows? We may not have been able to trace him along this line as the surname will have been lost... So, maybe, just maybe...

Eric Tebby

Eric Tebby was described to me as a "boxy little man." Actually that's how I remember him too, but with great affection. He always seemed to be wearing a brown knitted jumper. In his working life he was a maintenance engineer for cinema projection equipment and travelled all over the county. At weekends and school holidays his wife, Rene, and their son would go with him, taking an opportunity to walk on the beach if it was Sheringham cinema or out along the pier if Eric had to dash to Cromer.

He was an enthusiastic gardener. His own garden was magnificent, a riot of colour and perfume and he brought his skills to the garden at Goat Lane and to the grounds at the Gildencroft, until illness meant he could no longer handle a mower or a rake.

His ashes and those of Rene are buried together in the Gildencroft, in a sunny position to the immediate right as you come through the gate. There is a wooden seat, carved with his name, at the far end of the avenue of trees as a grateful memorial.

Undertaker

John Joseph Howes. D. 1946

John Howes is recorded on the record of burials in the Gildencroft as a builder and undertaker. He was a carpenter by trade and his home and business yard was in 27 Pottergate across the street from Goat Lane Meeting House.

He was introduced to Quakers through the Adult School classes and applied for membership with his wife Lucy Ann in 1886. They produced a large family of six girls and two boys. Archibald Charles who was born in 1894 lived only four months. Archibald Charles who was born in May 1896 lived a good life, surviving the First World War and moving to Essex afterwards. Arthur George joined his father in the building business.

6

Verse

Many of the Gurney daughters, sisters and cousins wrote their diary entries and letters between themselves in poetry. Some of it is striking; some of it certainly is not.

As part of the ongoing correspondence between the Joseph John Gurney and Amelie Opie, this is an extract of a missive written by Joseph in 1817:

… But most I love to mark devotion's flame
Rise from thy bosom in thy Maker's name:
Oh how I bless the ray of love divine
That first blew within thee, taught that flame to shine,
From mists of error drew they steps away,
And bade thee freely own a saviour's sway!…
Ah think again! That saviour bleeding see;
That thou might'st live to him he died for thee:
He died to save thee from a world of woe,
Tricked in the flippant pageantry of show…
Thine be the spirit willing to obey,
The faithful watching and the narrow way;
Thine be the Christian's daily cross to bear,
His labour and his burden thine to share!
Light is the burden, easy is the yoke,
Rest for thy soul, a meek redeemer spoke,
Rest for thy soul, and peace without alloy,
And overflowing balm, and everlasting joy.

W

Quaker Workhouse and the Warnes Family

In 1680 the Society of Friends, under the auspices of Six Week Meeting who had responsibility for the Society's buildings in the capital, began a scheme in East London whereby stocks of flax were purchased so that Quaker Poor could spin it both at home and in prison. The workhouse and school at Clerkenwell was intended to house 56 "decayed friends and orphans " with the elderly occupying one section of the house and the children in another employed in spinning mop yarn. Girls also made and mended inmates' clothing whilst boys learnt to read, write and cast account. Cold baths were offered to inmates "for their health and cleanliness. " Inmates brewed their own beer and the children helped with the preparation of the food.

Further plans formulated by John Bellers intended that this provision should increase to form a College of Industry, a Cooperative and Humanitarian Community for 200 labourers and 100 impotent poor. The emphasis was to be upon education and training done by object lesson rather than learning by rote. Inmates also had access to a library.

Though it could never replace the loving comforts of home this was not the Dickensian Workhouse of Oliver Twist. The diet was sufficient if somewhat monotonous by today's tastes. On First day they received two meals of bread, cheese and beer with a further dinner of 8 ounces of roast meat without bones and more beer. Second day brought more bread and cheese with milk and on the Third day their meat was "boyled". Fourth day served two meals of broth with a dinner of frumenty or rice milk. Fifth day was bread and cheese and "boyled" meat, Sixth alternated between "plumb" or plain pudding in the evening whilst the Seventh day saw a milk porridge or pease pottage. The children ate the same though in reduced portions and meals could be varied in seasons when there was a supply of peas, beans, mackerel, herring or salt fish.

The charge for country children was for boys 40/= entrance with 2/9d a week board and 10/= a quarter for clothing and 40/= entrance for girls with 3/6d board and 12/6 clothing. No reason is given for the difference other than if the boys could be found casual work outside they commanded a higher wage. A boy's labour was worth 1.= a week while the work done by the girls was valued at only twopence ha'penny. Norwich Meeting sponsored many of the Meeting's children over the years, some with parents some without. The remaining children of the Hitchen [qv] family, Jonathon and John were admitted. Diana Letchworth whose "husband is gone to America and hath left her and his Children unprovided for… requested that two of her children, Susannah and John, be placed in said Workhouse…" "Three children of Thomas Smith" were sponsored at the Workhouse School by Norwich Meeting "… in order to their being placed out as Apprentices…" [N.R.O. SF56]

Some families saw Clerkenwell as the best opportunity for their children and paid the fees themselves, many others were sponsored by their home Meetings or individual benefactors. Most of the children were found apprenticeships in London where it was believed there were more opportunities. [Clerkenwell Quaker Workhouse gradually evolved into Friends School, Saffron Walden.]

In May 1767, Samuel Warnes' wife approached Devonshire House Meeting, the closest to Clerkenwell, asking that her son Thomas "a boy about nine years old…" be admitted into the Workhouse. The Warnes Family had maintained two other children "in the said house, about four years but were not of the ability to continue that expence…".[N.R.O. SF56]

As Samuel was actually a member at Norwich, Devonshire asserted that Norwich should be responsible for the fees .

"Joseph Phipps and John Gurney Junior report that pursuant to the order of last Monthly Meeting they conferred with Samuel Warnes and several [London] friends… And that Samuel Warnes acquainted them, 'If this meeting would advance five pounds towards the putting out Apprentice his Eldest Son to himself, he should want no further Assistance from this Meeting at present'. Our Friends are desired to write to Some Member of Devonshire House, That if the Friends of said Monthly Meeting shall think him a proper Master for his Son and have him bound accordingly; this Meeting doth consent thereto and to pay the Five Pounds as requested…"

The fee was paid to Samuel Warnes and his son, Samuel Junior, legally became his apprentice. Thomas was given the place at Clerkenwell previously taken by Samuel. Samuel Warnes senior died possibly before the apprenticeship was complete. Minutes record that "The Widow Warnes" had sufficient of her own to defray Thomas's expenses. By 1773 Thomas was fifteen and had to leave Clerkenwell. He became apprentice to John Bousell, a Norwich cordwainer, [shoemaker] with Norwich Meeting paying the indenture fee of eight pounds.

> *"To the Committee of Friends School-house in Clerkenwell, London. Dear Friends, This is to acquaint you that Thomas Warnes, a boy lately discharged from your House is bound Apprentice to our Frd John Bousell of this City, Cordwainer who requesting to have five pounds as usually allowed by way of fee... [We] remain with the Salutation of Love your Friends and Bretheren, Norwich Monthly Meeting..."*

It was agreed that, as Thomas could live at home, the Meeting would pay one pound for board and lodging and sixteen shillings for his coach fare home.

A year later, Norwich elders ordered that the last Warnes boy at Clerkenwell, John, "... be placed at Board with his Uncle, Benjamin Warnes at 3/6d a week till further ordered; and the Overseers are desired to pay the expenses incurred by his removal from London, &c , And to supply him with such Wearing Apparel as they think necessary."

John Warnes lived the rest of his life in Norwich as a member of the Meeting, died at the comparatively early age of 39 in 1802 and was buried in the Gildencroft.

X-Certificate

John Lucas caused unease amongst Norwich Quakers and was spoken to by Elders;

> *... respecting his Conduct in several respects, particularly in attending Plays and Music Meetings as being contrary to ye Good Order and Discipline established amongst us, which he acknowledged to be just and seemed to take it in good part assuring [Friends] he would endeavour to behave for ye future in such a manner as not to give ye like Occasion again...*
>
> [N.R.O.SF55] Norwich Monthly Meeting 7th mo 1745

Christopher Pack

> *... in his way of life as a Portrait Painter [frequented] Places of Diversion...*
>
> [N.R.O. SF56] Norwich Monthly Meeting 10th Mo 1789

Eighteenth century Quakers gathered many things under their umbrella term "irregular practices". It could be anything. Eddington cites examples such as "irregular walking" this being consorting with unchaperoned unmarried women, "irregular worship" being consorting with Methodists, never mind sex outside marriage and the siring of illegitimate children.

Early nineteenth century Quaker books had to be passed by the Morning Meeting, a kind of censorship committee, before publication. Author Amelia Opie admitted that:

> *... novel reading as it is contemptuously called (and with some justice) has a tendency to make young persons disinclined to serious and more instructive reading & is therefore pernicious..."*

Nevertheless she argued she:

> *... never thought that works of fiction were never to be read, on the contrary, [she believed] simple moral tales the very best mode of instructing the young and the poor... Why did the blessed Saviour teach in parables?...*

1839 was still an era of disownments for 'Marrying Out' and lack of integrity in financial affairs, plain bonnets for the women, no lapels or pocket flaps on men's jackets. It was considered vainglorious in some households to have a looking glass or ornament their walls. So it is unsurprising that there are letters from J.J. Gurney expressing sympathy with his sister upon the refusal of her husband to make their children wear the distinctive Quaker dress.

Theatre, music and other entertainments did not sit comfortably with some Friends' scruples for a long time. Eddington selects a reference to the Norwich Music Festival premiering Spohr's Oratorio 'Calvary' whereby Anna Gurney writes to her father [J.J.]

> *... I suppose we shall not see Uncle Daniel [Gurney] and his daughters while it is going on as they will be quite taken up, and I am sure I do not wish to see more than I can help of the Norwich gaieties. I am glad to have my Quakerism to show, that puts it out of my possibilities to go to anything of the sort, for I cannot say that I approve of mixing up the Scriptures with amusements in this way; I had much rather go to a common concert. There is one, a new piece "Calvary", so shocking, that it seems to disgust everybody almost. Even Cousin Margaret told me she should not go...*

Elizabeth Fry's husband Joseph had a deep love of music that displeased his wife... "It had long been her sorrow...". She treated as a real affliction the fact that, as secular music was banished from his own home, he occasionally sought it at public concerts. He was even discovered to have been at the opera! She feared that any one of her daughters might be taken to a ball and so be subjected to and affected by such music. When this actually happened for one of them "... her sorrow knew no bounds..."

Rachel Fowler mentions in a letter to her father Joseph John Gurney how

> " ... *self denying [she has] been. There was at Norwich a famous man who was both "improvisator" and ventriloquist too, and most of*

us did certainly wish to hear him; however, seeing that he was conjurer too and rather theatrical, we gave it up to be on the safe side; Uncle Birkbeck was most kind but truly conscientious about it and he and I agreed that it was doubtful whether thou would have admitted such a visitor entertaining as he might be...".

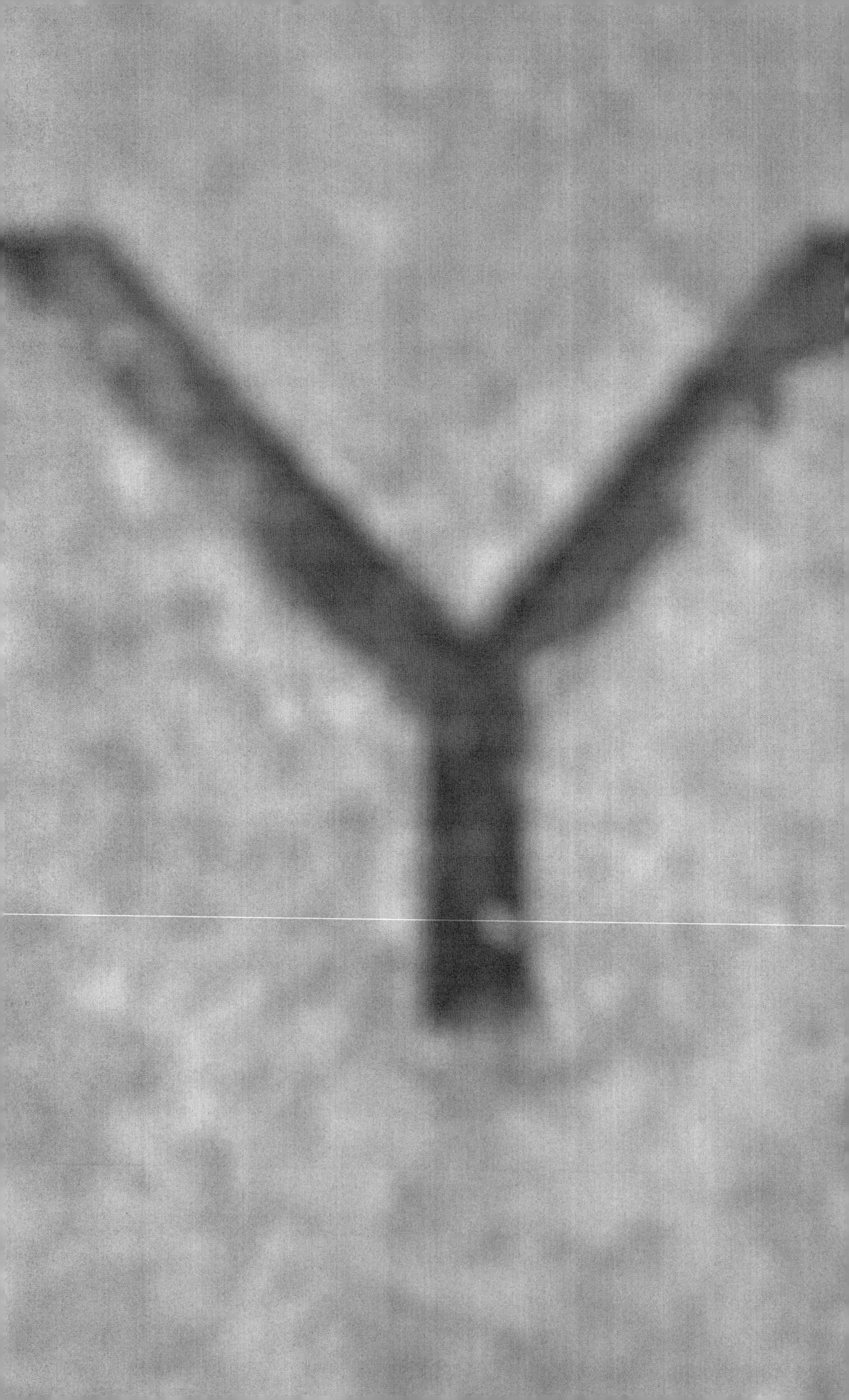

Young Friends

Quakers have always delighted in their children. If the family of a Young Friend was unable to care for them, it was often the Overseers of the Meeting that took on the responsibility.

Daughter of Hercules Williams 1750.

One Hercules Williams who frequented our Meetings and for some small time resided in this City have turned his Back of it & nor taken any care of, or provided for his Daughter whom he has left in a deplorable Condition. Being a Lunatick... [Friends] desire to know in what manner they would have us proceed...

Benjamin Fiddeman born 1707-8.

Benjamin, the epileptic son of John Fiddeman, deceased, despite all "his weaknesses and informitys..." was about to become twenty one. John Gurney was the executor of John's will, which had left the whole estate in trust to be handed to Benjamin when he was of age. There was concern within the Meeting that this might not be the wisest thing to have done, considering Benjamin might spend his legacy all in one go!

And that when the same may be spent he will be ye proper care of this Meeting. John Gurney is desired therefore to consult some proper security in order to lay out ye said money on an annuity for ye said Benjamin Fiddeman for Life...

Gurney's advice was to sink the inheritance into Corporation Bonds. Benjamin would receive "tenn pounds a year for his life and had received one hundred pounds in consideration thereof…".

Income assured for the young man, Friends were at pains to care for him and keep him well at all times. They came up with a mixed response. A minute agreed that:

Richard Taylor and Thomas Pain are desired to set near to Benjamin Fiddeman at our publick meetings and to do what in them lay to keep him awake in order to prevent his falling into fits…

Norwich Monthly Meeting 4th mo 1733

This might not have had the success they hoped for as a month later it was:

Ordered that the Doorkeepers provide a Chair in ye Meeting yard every afternoon on ye first day for Benjamin to set on during ye time of our afternoon meeting and they are further ordered to oblige him to keep out of ye meeting to prevent ye Disturbance which attends ye meeting by his frequent having of fits…

The Smart Family. 1765

Benjamin Smart's wife had lately died.

The necessitous Condition of Benjamin Smart's three Children being represented to this Meeting, our Women Friends are desired to take the necessary care…

Three weighty men Friends took charge to:

oblige their Father to contribute all in his power towards their Support & Maintainance… Two of [the children] are under the Care of his late Wife's sister [White] and that the third is with a Friend in the Country and that he at present pays toward their Maintainance Six Shillings a Week.

Benjamin failed to keep to the agreement, falling:

much short of his promise of paying Six Shillings… and has taken one of them home to himself there now remains One Child out at the expense of 1/6d a week and one other under the care of Women Friends…

Relief of the Poor

The Overseers of the Poor acquainted this Meeting that Isaac Ward's Children are in great Want of Clothing and that he is not of the ability to provide for them without the Assistance of Friends; the Overseers are therefore desired to provide what is necessary...

William Freake is reduced to so helpless a condition that one shilling per week is necessary to be added to his present allowance...

Bartholomew Blake being in great Want of Clothes, John Gurney is desired to give him £1.11.6d out of the Elizabeth Langwade Gift.[1]

Apprenticeships

If a Master ill-used his apprentice, Quakers were quick and able to petition the City's Mayor to have the indentures set aside and new indentures made. Benjamin, son of Thomas Hitchen and John, son of Isaac Ward were subject "to great misconduct on the part of the Masters...". The boys were found new Masters and their indentures continued[2]. Charles Drane was asked to take back his apprentice, William Ward "and do justice by him...". Drane made no improvement. Elders considered it "needful to obtain a proper discharge..." moving William to learn under Hammond Fisk for the remainder of his term[3].

For the love and help of the Meeting to continue towards its Young Friends, they in turn had to behave themselves. Isaac Swann was a Quaker apprentice. Sponsored with funds from the Elizabeth Langwade Gift and Samuel Robins' Trust, he had been accused by his Master James Millar of dishonesty and had absconded. "His conduct for a considerable time past [had] been very disreputable... frequenting of bad Company and too often falling into a state of intoxication... such baneful practices...". Elders desired that "he be brought to a conviction of the evil of his conduct".

The Roberts Family. 1780-1784.

The Roberts family were in a distressed necessitous situation. It seems that Mrs Roberts had died leaving Thomas Roberts unable to cope. According to the Elders' minutes the Roberts children were shiftless and the best thing to do was for their father, Thomas, to sell up and live with an-

1 N.R.O. SF56

2 N.R.O. SF56. Norwich Monthly Meeting 4th Month 1788

3 N.R.O. SF57. Norwich Monthly Meeting 9th Month 1790

other member of his family whilst the Meeting took over the care and education of the family.

> *And the four children at home with him we disposed of as follows; Elizabeth, the eldest, we procured a Service for in a Friend's house in Tottenham whither she is sent; Mary aged about 14 years is provided with a place at 1.6d per week; Susanna, aged about 12 years and Ann about 10 years are proposed to be sent to Ackworth School. Thomas Roberts readily agreed to pay seven shillings a week out of his earnings towards the support of his children…*

So it seems the young children would be all right, two with safe employment and two with a good education. Thomas, after a year, began to default on his payments with no excuse that he could give. His conduct was "such as calls for the care and oversight of this Meeting…". He was twelve shillings short. "We hope in time he will in a good degree remove the complaints alleged against him…"

Mary, in her placement "after several trials [was] still so refractory as to require the immediate notice of this Meeting… Women Friends to provide a proper place to put her in…". After some pains taken with her, Mary began to see the impropriety of her conduct. Annoyingly, the Minutes do not specify what her conduct was. The following month she was given a new place at a Friend's house and her conduct became "more satisfactory".

Rest In Peace

May perpetual light shine upon The faces of all who rest here.
May the lives they lived Unfold further in spirit.
May all their past travail Find ease in the kindness of clay.
May the remembering earth Mind every memory they brought.
May the rains from the heavens Fall gently upon them.
May the wildflowers and the grasses Whisper their wishes into light.
May we reverence the community of presence
In the stillness of this silent field.

John O'Donohue "On passing a graveyard"

Architect: David Percival A.R.I.B.A. 1917-1995

We record with sadness the sudden death of David Percival on 20th April 1995. David was a member of this Meeting for many years and was a much loved and respected Friend. In addition to his faithful attendance at Meetings for Worship and Business Meetings, we shall miss his great honesty, wisdom, eloquence, humour and generosity with his skills and his commitment to promoting the recognition of individual responsibility in public life as well as the care and maintenance of our individual Meeting Houses and many other public buildings in Norfolk.

Monthly Meeting Minutes 7th May 1995

David was Norwich City Architect from 1955 to 1974. Bombing in WW2 caused extensive damage to Norwich's housing stock. Much of its replacement, in both design and nature, came from him and his arguments in committee that no further multi storey blocks were desirable. He sought to provide good quality homes for those who could not have afforded to buy their own. In 1961 he received awards for the Midland Street redevelopment that consisted of 42 flats, 15 old peoples' bungalows, a hostel and a warden's house. He had won a similar award for the Anderson Place flats two years earlier[1]. Provision of the domestic housing stock continued throughout his tenure finishing with the St Leonards Road and Ladbrooke Place flats.

He oversaw the refurbishment and extension of City Hall and the Police Station in Bethel Street in the mid 1960s whilst guiding the team remodelling the Theatre Royal at the same time. Press reports of the theatre's reopening were joyous. Percival replaced "the white tiled frontage with a new image to get rid of what the critics had called the thirties public con-

1 Eastern Daily Press 22.4.95.

The old library on fire in 1994 (Photo by Sarah Cocke)

venience style…"

He designed and commissioned the new public indoor swimming pool at St Augustines, which was a great boon to residents and the city's economy in general. The pool, cited centrally, was in use eighteen hours a day, seven days a week by schools, clubs and individuals. Many important events were held there until both the roof and the pool itself were discovered to be leaking mainly caused by the structure of the land on which it had been built. This was at a time of stringent cuts to public funding nationally and the facility was forced to close. There was a great outcry in the press, "bad news/good news" cartoons lampooning the financiers, suggestions that there could be other activities up and down the emptied tiled slopes, each more idiotic than the last, until it was realised that its closure may reduce everyone's council tax bills by £73 a year. The City Fathers, together with Broadland District Council secured the provision of another pool, right out on the outskirts, which was connected to permission for a supermarket complex. Although well used, transport permitting, there has never been the affection that there was for St Augustines.

Percival served on the committee of the Historic Churches Trust. He was a classical violinist playing an active role in the Norwich Music Society. He was also a member of the Norwich Society. His wife, Mauny, described him as a lively man and great fun. "He carried out his work with great enthusiasm and he inspired the same enthusiasm in all those who worked with him…". He was a coordinator of Charter 88, a pressure group that advocated constitutional and electoral reform echoing the Chartist Movement of the mid 19th century.

David Percival is best remembered for the award winning design in the 1960s of the City Library on Bethel Street and Lady Lane. That gained him a bronze medal from the Royal Institute of Architects. At the time his work was judged to be the most outstanding building in Norfolk and the then Lord Mayor, Sidney Clapham, said Percival had "brought a welcome freshness of mind to Norwich." [E.D.P. op cit.] The Norfolk Records Office and a small lecture theatre were housed in the basement. Flat roofed, light and airy, faced in local flint work and arranged around a courtyard with a water feature in memory of those American servicemen who had flown out of local airfields during WW2, Percival's library became one of the most used public libraries in the country.

In 1990 it became obvious that more space was needed. By this time David had retired. The courtyard was roofed over, many partitions were taken down between departments and the whole layout and feel of the place changed. This was believed to be progress, what the readers wanted. Music departments were added. For those dinosaurs amongst us it became noisier, more bustling, less calm, but if the public were borrowing the books in the great numbers they were then this alteration must have been the right decision we were told.

Then in summer 1994 the library burnt to the ground. I stood, along with many other people of the city, and watched the efforts to save it. The fire services from all over the county laboured for three days, Percival said the open plan system (after alterations) had drastically altered the original intention of keeping the different sections of the library separate and made the fire worse. At the series of inquests a "County Hall Source" described the state of the library as appalling and said that Mr Percival would have been horrified at the deterioration of the building… A few pounds spent on wiring could have saved four million pounds, the biggest insurance claim by a local authority… [there had been] inadequate inspection…"

The following year, David died in hospital after a fall in the Cathedral Close but continues to be fondly remembered.

As an indication of how deeply he was involved with the work at Goat Lane, the business meeting of June 4th brought a further Minute:

> *"Minute 10. We ask Nominations to recommend a replacement for David Percival on Monthly Meeting Finance and Property Committee as well as Co ordinator of the Parliamentary Liason Group and to suggest a further name for the Monthly Meeting Nominations Committee to replace him as Elder."*

“I sat next to him one Wednesday lunch,” says one Friend. “I had no idea who he was at first. He had a beard and he was retired, he said. He was genial enough. Equally, I had no idea that he had had such a phenomenal role in the estates around Norwich. He kept his light hidden under a bushel. He made decent houses for decent people as part of his Quaker testimonies and social conscience. His work was a practical expression of his Quaker values.”

B

The Bidwell Family

There are ten members of the Bidwell family buried in the Gildencroft. Henry Bidwell, born 1785, was a prominent citizen with a general grocery and agency on Exchange Street and a house on Lakenham Terrace in the Bracondale area. Influential people like the Gurneys also had homes in this area. In his mid twenties Henry and his beloved wife Elizabeth produced their first child, a son they named Henry Junior. In the summer of 1811 they were doubly blessed with their second son, Thomas Edward, and in early 1813 their daughter Eliza was born. The happiness of the young couple must have seemed complete.

Chase's Norwich Directory 1783, around the time of Henry's birth, records that the city had six physicians and twenty surgeons; including five surgeon apothecaries, two surgeon druggists and a man midwife, their collective numbers only increasing slightly by 1830 when his own youngest children were born. Norwich's vaccination programme began in 1805 and helped to restrict the 1819 smallpox epidemic in the city but even so, sanitation, antenatal care and midwifery then were not as we take for granted today, neither was there the universal availability of medicines and modern antibiotics. Crosse (Variolous Epidemic) records that during the decades before and after the 1831 cholera outbreak "between 1500 and 1600 people had been attacked by smallpox, measles, scarlet fever and typhus."

It can be seen, therefore, that the smallest infection could develop into a tragedy.

In the early winter of 1814 Thomas Edward died aged only three and a half years old. Six days later Elizabeth Bidwell died, leaving Henry without a wife and two small children without a mother. Two weeks after her death, baby Eliza died. Henry and his remaining small son must have spent a bleak Christmas examining their faith. How could this have been the will of a caring God?

John Birkbeck 1845. Æt. 48.
John Kiddle 1771. Æt. 72
not known
Benjn Gurney 1750. Æt. 57
Elizth Birkbeck 1836. Æt. 22 yrs.
Ann White 1788. Æt. 68.
Bartlett Gurney 1803. Æt. 47.
Mary Gurney 1810. Æt. 65.
Anthony White 1775. Æt. 73.
Sarah Gurney 1764. Æt. 68.
Hannah wife of Bartlett Gurney
Frances Tennant 1833. Æt. 55.
Francis Dix 1902 Æt. 88
Hannah Chapman 1795. Æt. 80
Mary Gurney 1810. Æt. 84
Elizabeth Dix 1881 Æt. 80
Mary Lance 1784. Æt. 83
Ann Holt 1814. Æt. 47
Elizth Mary Lloyd 1829. Æt. 58.
Thos. Hart 1750. Æt. 40
Sophia Bland 1818. Æt. 14½
not known
Anna Forster 1855. Æt. 70.
not known
David Lloyd 1839 Æt. 69.
Elizth Hart 1750. Æt. 56
not known
Rachel Gurney 1825. Æt. 62
Rachel Gurney
Mary Sparks 1770. Æt. 17
Catherine Gurney 1792. Æt. 38.
Martha Birkbeck 1822. Æt. 74

The burials index (actual physical cards in a box) which has been compiled from the burials map, which in turn was drawn from somewhat haphazard eighteenth and early nineteenth century record keeping. Bidwell himself in his later life would have been one of those compilers. The map, now in its third edition drawn in the 1850s, is on a linen paper roll kept wrapped around a wooden core with carved finials. It is stored safely in a metal cylinder at Goat Lane Meeting House so that each new interment can be recorded. Coffin shapes are drawn in scratchy pen and ink, some inks having lasted better than others, until those most recent burials are in obvious modern pen. Most shapes have names. Many are tiny; so tiny that the person whose coffin it is might have not lived long enough to have been given a name.

Consultations with our Keeper of Archives suggest that in the case of the Burials Ledger "old entries were transcribed from scribbles, literally in some cases, on envelopes and hung together with string. Wouldn't be allowed these days!" she says emphatically. " [And] whoever made the record sometimes couldn't write nor spell and most of the information would have been gathered orally hence the variations of spelling..." Her expression is one of apologetic despair.

But these failings on the part of past information gatherers leave Bidwell open to a degree of unwarranted misconstruing...Henry married again, very soon, actually so soon that based on the dates given below for Edward I can't make the time add up!

Henry and Mary Ann, who was eight years Elizabeth's junior, smartly produced a son, Edward Thorpe. Gildencroft records show that this Baby Edward died in the third week of January 1816 aged one year. The family produced no more recorded babies until a stillborn son in July 1823, followed by Lewis in October 1824 who sadly died aged only eleven days old. After due mourning perhaps the small family could enjoy some time together. Another Edward was born in 1827, Eliza [another Eliza] was born in the summer of 1829 and Anna arrived at the end of July 1830. Henry now had four living children. Happy days.

Baby Anna died two weeks after her birth.

In the autumn of 1832, Henry and Mary Ann's last child, Charles, was born. He lived little more than two years. Edward died six months later. After all this anguish, Henry had one surviving child from each of his wives. Henry Junior left the Society in 1851 possibly by marrying a woman who was not a member and so forfeiting his membership. Quakers are not faced with this decision today. Eliza married a Mr Goultry and lived in Saffron Walden where she unfortunately died aged only thirty-four.

It is interesting to have an insight into how nineteenth century Quakers were perceived by outsiders. Henry Bidwell is mentioned in this account by two guests at a wedding at Goat Lane. As Meeting Clerk he would have been the master of ceremonies, the 'Grand Manager'. He seems to have had the whole event under control. The bride was Anna, daughter of Joseph John Gurney and her groom was John Church Backhouse.

> *"We have all been at Anna Gurney's wedding this morning... so hemmed in by the crowd of persons that attended... The wedding was to be at eleven o clock, we reached the Meeting House at Goat lane by a quarter past ten but found little choice of seats. Mr Bidwell who seemed to be grand manager as to order appeared uneasy at the increasing concourse and said it would be impossible to proceed if one of the aisles was not cleared. By some means sufficient room was made for a procession to advance so as to reach their appointed seats..."*
>
> Sarah Glover

> *"There was such a crowd that we could scarcely see anything of the party and it was not easy to hear as the peculiar accent of Friends is not very intelligible to strangers. We had very bad places at the Meeting but got into the little lobby afterwards and so just saw most of the party. I was not a little amused by hearing the carriages announced in what I heard you describe as ballroom style. Sir Fowell stalked in shouting 'The Grove carriage', 'The Edward Buxton's carriage' &c. There must have been a long train of carriages..."*
>
> Christiana Bird

Henry Bidwell was now totally on his own and sought refuge and strength in his work with Norwich Meeting. In April 1851 he was approached by Joseph Massingham from a local Methodist congregation to lease the Goat Lane Meeting House which, since its completion in 1826, had been a drain on Quakers' resources. Bidwell saw this as a way to get the Meeting out of financial hardship. The Religious Census earlier in the year had shown that, next to Anglicans, Methodists nationally had the strongest congregations and so needed a central place to worship.

Bidwell wrote asking the advice of Samuel Gurney who was living in London managing the City offices of Gurneys Bank.

"Thou art aware of the difficulties in our Monthly Meeting rendering the accommodation far beyond our wants and our diminished resources... Knowing the interest that thou takes in all that concerns the Society in Norwich I am induced to trouble you with this..."

Gurney approved the idea of selling Goat Lane even though this indicated "a sad change in Norwich, a locality where my family have for so many years met for so solemn a purpose… [and] the rapid falling away of all in which I have a deep interest. I trust we may profit by the reform…".

Bidwell offered Massingham a freehold for £3,500. This, remember, was the building that had cost Norwich Quakers £7,500 only a quarter of a century before. It is not recorded why the deal was not pursued.

The kinship within the Society of Friends must have been of great comfort to Henry. He was Clerk to Norwich Meeting for nearly three decades, which was how he came to be embroiled in the search for William Spicer Crowe. The Society looked after its own, so long as it remained deserving.

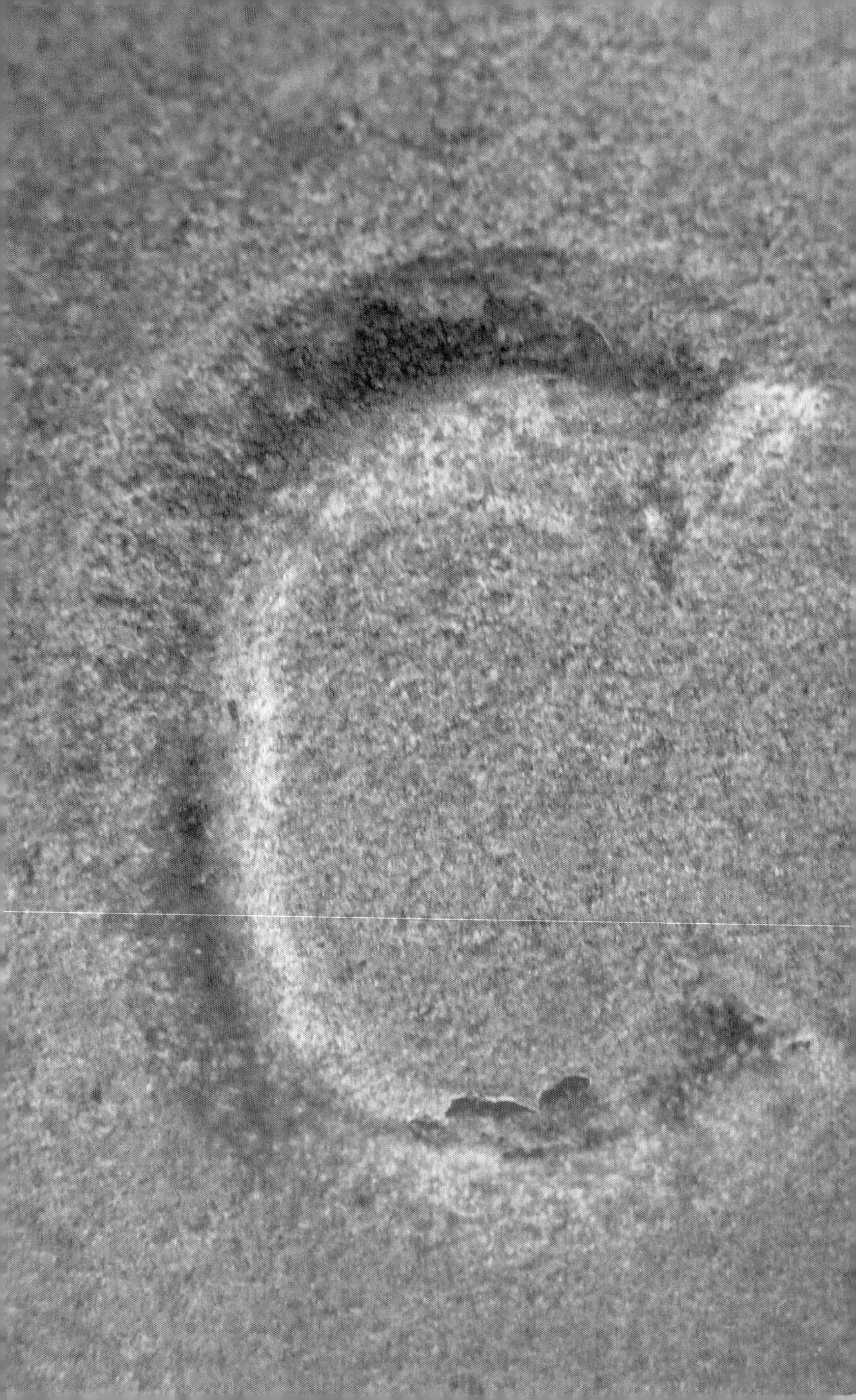

The Crowe Family

As early as 1765 Crowes became caretakers or wardens at the Meeting House. In May of that year it was decided that "a William Crowe and Wife be admitted to dwell in the House belonging to the New Meeting House until further ordered, and they would be allowed one shilling per week to keep the Meeting House clean and in good order...." Friends were asked to get the said Dwelling House put into order as soon as they conveniently could.

Crowe declined the offer. It was left for Friends "to consider of a proper Person for the same". No one else wanted the job so Crowe finally agreed "to go into the Dwelling adjoined to the New Meeting House... on condition that the usual Allowance is discontinued...." They would do the job for no payment. They were "desired to remove thereinto as soon as he can with convenience..." and carried on in this arrangement until 1774.

Crowe felt a call to Travel in the Ministry, solemnly laying "... before the Meeting a concern which has for some time rested on his Mind to pay a Religious Visit to Friends in Lincolnshire, Cambridgeshire, Huntingdonshire and some parts of Hertfordshire and places adjacent". His journey did not go quite as planned. Although he expressed his satisfaction to the Meeting on his return and reported that he had enjoyed the companionship of Joseph Ransome therein "having been taken ill on his first entrance into Lincolnshire he found freedom to decline proceedings in that country."

William Spicer Crowe

The firm of Mary Crowe and Sons, Plumbers and Glaziers of St Benedicts in Norwich were Quakers of long standing and had been one of the main contractors for the Goat Lane Meeting House , described in the newspapers at its opening in 1826 as "the most handsomest and commodious modern building in the city". Spicer Crowe (and possibly his father William before him) had a history of money "irregularities" . Minute books record Friends' concerns about reports of Spicer seeking work and "the high life" in other parts of the country and eventually, mindful of the good name of the Society, he was rescued from bankruptcy by some of the Meeting at the eleventh hour. For this reason his name no longer appeared on the firm's letter headings, and this he greatly resented.[1]

Both Mary (mother of Spicer and so Grandmother of William Spicer) and Spicer's wife Martha died during 1850 engaging Spicer in much expense to the detriment of the firm's finances. Young William had been expected to keep the work going by himself. It was not an occupation he relished; after all, he had had a good education. He abandoned his family and took off to London to seek a fresh start. He had no money from Spicer who himself again awaited financial help from the Meeting.

Young William attended some Meetings for Worship at Chelsea and after a time applied for his membership to be transferred from Norwich. The usual character references were sought. Robert Alsop there, Bidwell's opposite number wrote that William had obviously been

> *...backsliding. I [Alsop] spoke to him [William] and told him that our Meeting would not accept him unless he were in attendance. [William] told me that he would be at meeting the next First Day but did not attend in the morning being so tired with his work... He called here about two weeks since and told me that he was quite out of heart with the business, that he had been only yesterday seeking work unavailingly. Unless he got employ before the end of the week he would enlist in the army...*

It was the early 1850s and things were about to come to a head in the Crimea. Quakers saw, and still see, peace as a common concern for all Christians and the incompatibility of war with religion. It is recorded in our Minute Book for the time:

> *Friends are faithful in bearing our Christian testimony against*

1 Spicer Crowe has left a lead plaque fixed to the queen post in the roof of Goat Lane Meeting House with his name and date picked out in dots by a hammer and nail. Traditionally many tradesmen sign their work but here it seems that as his name did not appear as a director of the firm he was anxious to mark his part in the project. The plaque is still there but requires a vertiginous climb to see it.

bearing arms and being in any manner concerned in the militia, in privateer or armed vessels...

N.R.O. SF62

Meeting For Sufferings (17th January 1854) remained restrained in its Epistle of :

...much religious concern in contemplating the apparent probability of war between some of the nations of Europe.

Three weighty Quakers, Joseph Sturge, a Birmingham corn merchant, Robert Charleton, a pin manufacturer from Bristol and Henry Pease the railway magnate were sent by Sufferings to plead with the Czar in St Petersburg.

There are those in England who desire thy temporal and spiritual welfare as sincerely as thine own subjects do....

The trip sparked a furore in and outside the Society, some Friends arguing that the three were intent upon their own glorification. The press, however, believed the men's sincerity though called them misguided and naïve, but the Russian troops were already amassed and the Czar considered it was too late to recall his generals.

In this climate the two Clerks, Alsop in London and Bidwell in Norwich, were naturally horrified. Here was this young man, William Spicer Crowe brought up as a Quaker, seemingly intent upon joining the army. But to William the prospect of a warm coat and dry boots with three meals a day must have made the Sapper's life seem better than his present hand to mouth existence. Whatever was the true purpose of the young man's challenge it worked as Alsop's correspondence with Bidwell continued.

I gave him a letter to a painter whom I have myself employed, [who] gave him employment...

William was found to be very slow but this did not discourage his employer who gave him another chance the next day. However instead of being at his work at six o' clock William did not arrive on site until nine in the morning. The paperhangers were "quite thrown out by him" so he was discharged. William called at Alsop's house saying "his means were quite exhausted..." and talked of going abroad if he could get money.

Alsop recommended a return to Norwich where the young man was known. William was determined never to do this and blamed his father for bringing him into a trade he never liked. Alsop summed up Crowe's problems to Bidwell "I cannot but fear that idleness is at the bottom of his troubles..." but nonetheless advanced the young man five shillings on the understanding that it would be repaid. Norwich Friends set up a fund with London Friends for William to draw upon and by mid September that year one pound had been handed over in instalments.

Alsop wrote to Bidwell again:

> *The ten shillings I gave him last week went towards arrears at his lodgings and five shillings for his suppers and he is now without a farthing. He is determined to enter the Sappers and Miners....all that he wants is to get to Woolwich. Of course I cannot advance it for this as it is a military camp but I intend to hand him 2s 6d for his sustenance until I hear what is to be done...*

William argued (so that he might not be thought against the Quaker Peace Testimony) that the Sappers and Miners were engaged upon government work in that they had begun the Ordinance Survey mapping work and were men of superior character, intellect and dedication. That the mapping had been started for military purposes caused the conflict. Alsop replied to Bidwell.

> *...I cannot get him to attend our Meetings; he has some excuse and says he does not much like them. I am done with the poor young man...*

Henry Bidwell took a heavy and uncompromising approach with William, a boy he must have watched grow, through the Meeting, to manhood.

> *...I am truly grieved to hear of the very pitiable state to which thou appear to be reduced...I am far more grieved at the self indulgence...If thou art determined to take this course, thou must, but thou will have only thyself to blame for the consequences...*

Bidwell had lost most of his own family; he wasn't going to let this young man go under without one final try.

> *...If despairing of overcoming in this country the inveterate habits which have brought thee to ruin, thou could emigrate... something could be done to assist thee...*

Arrangements were made for Alsop to visit Crowe but it seemed he had left to seek work in Reigate. Unfortunately this was a disappointingly short stay with no work forthcoming. By March 23rd 1852 Crowe "…was expecting to get work in a few days and would probably go down to Brighton." The money Norwich had left with Alsop had run out again, indeed it was twelve shillings and sixpence overdrawn. Bidwell felt "an extreme difficulty."

Friends' wide and enduring networks gave every opportunity for help to those in need, irksome though Crowe obviously found it. At the beginning of May 1852 he had supposedly been working in Hertfordshire. Determined to find him, Alsop on behalf of Bidwell,

> *…enquired at a coffee shop in Exeter Street where I was told that he had left four or five shillings on their books… They expect him back again as he has left some of his things. It is two or three weeks since he left them. I had reason to believe he is in the habit of indolence to which all his prospects are sacrificed… The baker told me that his not getting any work was in consequence of his not getting up in the mornings…*

William still absented himself from any Meetings for Worship but received frequent financial assistance "such as thought needful…." Word reached Norwich that the young man was about to leave London with no fixed destination and the Meeting realised that there was nothing more they could do for him. Disownment was inevitable.

> *…We hereby declare that we no longer acknowledge him as a member of our Religious Society. At the same time we feel an earnest desire that….he may be preserved from the dangers to which he is exposed….. and be led to walk in the path of obedience and self denial…..not slothful in his business…..serving the Lord.*

William's sister Mary made a stand on behalf of her brother. One month after he was disowned in absentia she resigned her own membership of the Society. There are sixteen members of the Crowe family buried in the Gildencroft; the young Mary is not one of them.

On 28th March 1854 war in the Crimea was declared. One young soldier wrote home to his father

> *…This is a very cold country but we have had very little snow. I hope please the Lord that we shall soon make a shift from here… We have lost a great many men since we came from England. What with*

the fighting and the cholera together there is very few of them left. But thank God I have been very lucky so far...

Letter from Daniel Anguish, Ist Battalion Colstream Guards, camp before Sebastopol, 10th March 1854[2]

It is not known what became of William Spicer Crowe nor where he is buried; it is to be hoped that he is not amongst those young men killed in their thousands in the desperate cold of the Crimea.

The Casseretto Family

R.H. Mottram writes

...that a colony of Italian immigrants established themselves in Ber Street. Coming from their overcrowded poverty stricken land, I suppose to them it seemed paved with gold...

Described variously as café proprietors and refreshment caterers, there are four members of the Casseretto family buried in the Gildencroft.

October 23 1897.

To The Clerk of the Norwich Monthly Meeting of the Society of Friends.

Dear Sir

Having attended the meetings of the society of Friends for upwards of eight years and feeling that is my home and that the distinguishing views held by them are very much my own I should like to be united in membership with them

Yours truly Francis George Casseretto

That's it. A small sheet of cheap paper and a rough pen nib. One sentence, two spelling errors, one long word with not enough room left on the line so that it spills over onto the next and a couple of smudges. It speaks of great effort almost as if it has been much prepared beforehand and he has spent a whole evening copying it out. But it is correctly addressed and the script is painstaking.

The following report is brought in by the Friends appointed to visit Francis George Casseretto on his application for membership viz:- We have had an agreeable interview with Fran. Geo. Casseretto relative

2 N.R.O./MC20/40/3

to his application for membership. His parents (now both deceased) were Roman Catholics and he was brought up as such. Soon after his attendance at the Lads School to which he had been introduced by the late Richard Alden (who was then its Superintendent) he says he became enlightened to see that religion was a more spiritual thing than he had before understood. He continued for a time to attend the Roman Catholic Chapel but when he was at more liberty to choose for himself, he attended our Meetings which he has continued to do for about 8 years, the mode of Worship adopted by Friends having his approval. He is also generally in accordance with our distinguishing views in other respects. We have no hesitation in recommending his application to the favourable consideration of the Monthly Meeting.
William Newby. Henry Brown.

This report is approved by the Meeting and Francis George Casseretto is hereby recorded a member of our religious Society. H. Brown is requested to inform him.
Norwich Monthly Meeting 11th Month 1897

Arguably, Norwich Quakers in the nineteenth century allowed their strength and membership to become reduced by remaining insular and dilatory, failing to reach out to the community around them. Efforts to increase numbers were few until new families began coming to Goat Lane, attracted by the classes in the Adult and First Day Schools. The old families, the dynasties like the Gurneys had gone, "married out", taking the

underpinning wealth and experience with them. These new young families were modern and in trade and aware of changing times in society in general.

Francis Casseretto, with the family home in one of the small courts off Ber Street, was the keeper of one of the temperate Quaker Coffee Carts stationed at various points about the city, aimed primarily at the cattle drovers bringing their beasts to market in front of the castle.

Daniel Casseretto, Francis's son started a football team. Did you know Goat Lane Meeting once had its own football team in a local league. I certainly didn't!

We thank Michael Cullingford for the loan of the photograph. Michael's own great grandfather, also in the picture, became a member of the Society about the same time as Francis having moved from Ipswich to Lowestoft where he founded the Pakefield Quaker Mission which still meets today.

Diplomat

Liao Hongying 1905-1998. H. Derek Bryan 1910-2003

Hongying and Derek Bryan share a headstone in the Gildencroft. It is the only one extant that deviates from the usual Quaker pattern in that her name is also sculptured in Chinese characters.

Liao Hongying was born in Changting, a small town in southern China. This was the end of the Chinese Empire; she then lived through the Republic of Sun Yatsen, the Warlords, Chiang Kaishek, the Civil War to the foundation of the Peoples' Republic, seeing her country emerge finally as an independent modern state.

The Liao family was poor in a material sense but revered book learning. The men of the household were Confucian scholars, their father's writing and teaching bringing in the family's income while the women did the household chores, cooking, sewing and embroidery, laundry and cleaning. Her mother, it is reported, had wanted another boy. Hongying, the youngest child, with her strong will and intellectual curiosity, refused to conform to those gender patterns. Throughout her whole life she disliked and avoided housework.

Her father had given his daughter a love of Chinese classical writings from an early age. On the birthday of Confucius he would wear his robes, embroidered with dragon and phoenix and go to the temple at midnight. Girls then were not generally considered worth educating. He enrolled Hongying in a Missionary School which brought her into contact with western ideas and history, planting seeds of revolution that would be with her for the rest of her life.

"This sealed her destiny," writes her close friend and biographer Innes Herdan. It ensured "that she would spend the rest of her life between China and England, never quite coming to rest… This is evident in the way she uses language… her English husband speaks Chinese with ease….” but Hongying “uses sometimes both in the same sentence…”[1]

She had no pens, which were modern and expensive. As a schoolgirl Hongying wrote with the traditional brush and ink stick ground up with water. One of her brothers later bought her a slate. In the last year of Primary School she became a boarder. It was her teacher, Marjorie Rainer who wouldn't let her continue to live at home as there seemed never to be enough to eat. In the holidays Hongying was always hungry. The boys were allowed steamed eggs but Hongying was only given chestnuts, as this was all a girl was worth. She was often ill at school and the second time her mother ever came out of their house was to visit her daughter.

There was no secondary education for girls in her home town so, aged fourteen she was promoted to class teacher, a responsibility she carried for five years and during this time her beloved father died. She was then considered old enough to leave home to continue her own education. A place was found for her at an American Missionary School two days journey away on foot across the mountains and a further twelve days by small riverboat. At night in the dormitory she led much discussion with the other girls; politics, intellectual subjects, logic.

By 1926, the general struggle in China was deepening. There were reports of soldiers looting, supposedly on behalf of the people, in opposition to the levies and taxes by the Warlords. Hongying and two companions in the Students Union representing their school went into the streets, marching and speaking on street corners to explain to the citizens the meaning of the approaching revolution. For Hongying this was “an exciting time…” On 12th April 1927, in Shanghai, workers and young people were massacred in their thousands by armed gangsters working for the right wing Chaing Kaishek. Out of fear for their own safety the students undertook no more organised political activities and she concentrated her efforts on studying for entrance to Beijing University to read mathematics.

The whole county knew of the Liao family, her father as a Confucian teacher, Hongying as an activist. Fear grew and her eldest brother, now head of the family, wanted her to go away for the safety of them all. Marjorie Rainey arranged, and provided the funds, for Hongying to travel to London, live with some friends of hers then go to an English university.

She arrived in London, “a city colder than she had ever known in China…” with completely unsuitable clothing.

She lodged on the south coast with two unmarried women in “a house always neat and clean with plenty of china ornaments which seemed use-

1 All quotations from Fragments of a Life. I. Herdan. Larks Press 1996.

less to Hongying… Her home had had only the essentials." Because their boarder hadn't come from a Christian family the women imposed Bible lessons on Hongying. One woman, a Congregationalist, and the other Church of England made a special plea for her to be allowed to attend services.

To be closer to her education, Hongying moved into a hostel in London and continued to work towards Matriculation as a first step towards university entrance. In the capital, she met Harry Sillcock, a Quaker who invited her with others to his house at Jordans for weekends. On one occasion she asked to attend a Quaker Meeting for Worship.

> *Great was her surprise to find the 'church' was just a simple room and the 'service' merely a silence. There were no set hymns or prayers, no hierarchy, anybody could speak or pray and especially no 'up and down' as she called it. In a very short time she realised 'this is my place…*

Hongying selected Somerville College at Oxford to which to make an application. Unlike some other colleges it seemed to profess no particular faith. She took up her place in October 1930, meeting Innes soon after her arrival. She learned to manoeuver a punt, to ride a bicycle but found that of the ninety chemistry students admitted that year to the whole of Oxford University, only seven were women. She joined the Labour Club, the Communist Club, the United Nations Association and a dancing club which met in the Quaker Meeting House. She found the academic work "comparatively dull…" especially for someone who was concerned about social change. She told her Principal, Helen Darbishire that she wanted to leave college and go to Russia. Darbishire advised her to consult Lord Lindsay, Master of Balliol "for he is a wise person and very knowledgeable about those countries…" Lindsay was sympathetic but advised her that her heart was still in China and that would be where her future lay.

In 1934, Hongying took her Chemistry finals and upon passing was offered a post back in China, at Wuhan University to be in charge of soil analysis. In preparation for her acceptance she took further studies at University College, Aberystwyth, Rothampsted and Glasgow and by the summer of 1936 she was ready to return to China.

Music stayed with Hongying all her life: one of her greatest pleasures was listening to choral singing and orchestral playing, watching players and conductors. She was especially fond of the organ. Her high school teacher at Nanchang had encouraged her to specialise in music for which she undoubtedly had a gift, learning to play the piano to a high standard.

She wouldn't hear of music as a career; that would be self indulgent.

> *China is a vast country and there are natural calamities almost every year. The people need food so I must help improve the agriculture...*

Her heart was dedicated to her home country.

Innes joined her at Wuhan with the intention of becoming a classical translator. She recalls that although the two women had fun together living in halls of residences, Hongying did not really enjoy the life there. There was no sophistication, no urban life then. Her Oxford experiences meant that she did not mix well with the rest of the faculty who, in the main, had been educated in America.

The university had been put in charge of the forestry and crops along the Wuhan to Beijing railway. Hongying loved this project, writing back to Innes "I am born a vagabond and irresponsible. I love to be clean cut off... to live a community life [rather than a home life]... Even this dirty train is better than our nunnery...."

In 1937 the Japanese occupied Beijing and were advancing south. Wuhan University abandoned its campus and Innes returned home for safety. Hongying stayed where she was and was one of the last to leave. All her papers, belongings and soil samples were lost in the enemy bombing. Innes records that she understood Hongying to be "unspeakably sad and lonely..." Again she was marooned in a strange place with none of the right clothing.

She found lodgings with the Zheng family at Guiyang. Although they were kind to her, Mrs Zheng would help herself to Hongying's groceries and rats bit at her toes during the night. She wanted to remain active so began to teach at the local High School. Her class was of 80 to 90 little boys, were disorderly and the lack of English textbooks meant that she had to teach by actions and mime. It was satisfying enough but she longed to return to University level. Wuhan University had now re established itself in Kiating in Sichuan province and Hongying secured herself a post. As a single woman she had a hard struggle to find herself somewhere to live, writing back to Innes in England "Sometimes the heart is so sad that the brain becomes dull and the mouth dumb...." Sometimes she felt that China was almost lost; she herself felt heartsick. There was compulsory military training for all students and she resigned.

Hongying contacted William Sewell, the Quaker head of the department of Chemistry at the West China Union University at Chengdu who later became a good friend of hers to say she was available for teaching.

She took the offered post but it did not fulfil her hopes or expectations… "The students are like clay and wooden images. They do the textbooks and nothing else. I have been trying to move things a little bit and in consequence I offend everyone. You know I have no tact. So the sum total is despair…".

She helped to organise Bible study groups and Hymn singing. Secretly they also discussed Marxism reading communist literature behind closed curtains. A friend of hers who went to Chengdu in 1979 and visited the Museum of this University saw there a note to the effect that Liao Hongying is a dangerous person and has to be watched!

After four years at Chengdu, Harry Sillcock arrived from London to organise a post war conference on behalf of the Quakers. He engaged Hongying to be the Organising Secretary with Sichuan Quakers being responsible for her salary. It wasn't paid so she moved on to Chongqing, taking a room in the decrepit YMCA and was joined for a time by the Zheng family. She worked with the Sino-British Co operation office in the British Embassy compound that had been set up by Joseph Needham whom she had known at Cambridge but became ill and weak from poor living conditions and lack of nourishing food. There wasn't much food for anyone in China at that time but for those without a family around them it was far worse. Needham was preparing to travel to Lanzhou and further Universities. He persuaded Hongying to travel with him as Chongqing seemed to him to be the source of her illness. The government was sponsoring the truck and the break could only but do her good. Hongying agreed.

At Lanzhou Needham heard that the British Consul from Chengdu was visiting and he suggested that they jointly pay him a courtesy call in the China Inland Mission. Herdan records…"'Call on an imperialist official – not likely,' exploded Hongying…" Needham tried to persuade her saying they had only to leave a calling card but she was adamant. At one of Needham's meetings some days later the young British Consul was sitting in front. Hongying thought he was one of the missionaries. At a meal later she was introduced to the Consul, Derek Bryan for the first time. He was a Diplomat, she realised, not a Missionary.

Needham decided to fly back to Chongqing leaving the rest of his party to return in the government truck. Derek Bryan, who had flown to Lanzhou initially, joined the party going by road. One night on the journey Hongying's cough kept them all awake. Next morning, Derek produced a bowl of traditional Chinese cough remedy which Hongying found comforting. It was a long journey but she gradually improved. Derek looked after her all the time putting his coat over her to keep her warm. The truck, held together with lengths of string, kept breaking down and at one repair stop the couple's conversation convinced Hongying that he was not an Imperialist after all but "on the side of the people…". After that they talked freely in the truck and when they reached Chengdu she gave him some dried Hami melon, a great delicacy.

Once the couple had known each other for some time Derek asked Hongying to marry him. She said that she was too old for him. "'I intend to live and die in China,' she stated." Derek must not ruin his Diplomatic career because of her. Nevertheless on 16th June 1944 they married, in the manner of Quakers at West China University in Chengdu. Derek's leave was due and they left for England, via Calcutta and Gibraltar sitting on the floor of an R.A.F. flying boat, arriving into an England of wartime rationing.

Derek's father was a respected Norwich dentist with a house on the outskirts of the city. There was domestic help in the family but Hongying felt she wanted to help. She attempted to do things like washing up but items got broken; she attended to the family beds but this was unwelcomed. Life for her was a real cultural shock. Gradually the relationships eased and before she died Mrs Bryan was recorded as saying that she could not have had a better daughter in law.

Hongying and Derek took a holiday in the English Lake District, meeting up with Innes and her new husband and two children. Innes recalls that Hongying would, "in a sense of scientific inquiry", wonder why she had lost some of her spirit, her industriousness and independence. She was troubled that she left Derek to handle their money and buy their stamps! Had Innes found this was usual in newly married women? Was it temporary or permanent?

Derek's leave was cut short; he was needed back in London by the Foreign Office. They found a place to stay with Marjory Fry. Hongying's domestic chores were a trial to her. She had believed that married women in Britain would have a better life than their counterparts in China. This did not seem to be so! She was given a post with the British Council in the China Section.

At the end of the war, Derek was offered a position as Chinese Secretary at the British Embassy and the couple returned to China. Their hope was that Derek's belongings that had been in storage in Macao would be waiting and useable. Much of it was damaged and they gave a great deal of it away. Hongying would dearly have liked to visit her family but there was still banditry and little peace between Chiang Kaishek and Mao Zedong. Travelling was difficult. The social life within the Diplomatic service was awkward for her with many cocktail parties at which she was expected to accompany her husband but they made many friends, both Chinese and foreign.

Hongying became known for being generous though outspoken and a lover of political discussion. Around this time, students began to demonstrate and demand a good education: society began to collapse. Young people "disappeared" at night. However they spent a fruitful and exciting year under a Charge d'Affaires in Nanjing. Although ordinary communications were cut off and they were not allowed to travel outside city limits there was plenty of new life, new films, new theatre.

In 1950, British diplomatic staff moved to Beijing. Hongying joined a Study group of Chinese women, wives of professional people who discussed American Imperialism and the United Nations. This gave her some degree of stimulus. The following year, travelling became freer and the couple took home leave in Norwich once more. The usual rule was that a Diplomatic Officer whose wife was not British should not be posted to her home country. As this had not been followed in their 1946 posting they were confident of a return to China. The Foreign Office said that Derek had become to pro Chinese and Hongying too anti American, and instead offered him a post in Peru - Derek opted for early retirement.

They set up home in a rented flat in North London. Derek attended classes in Classical Chinese at the school of Oriental and African Studies intending to do some Sinological research. Two years later came a move to the quiet of Cambridge where Derek could work towards a PhD. Hongying still hated domestic work dreading the drudgery of it all. They began speaking engagements together; United Nations Associations, Townswomens' Guilds, Trades Unions Branches. She felt these engagements were impinging upon Derek's studying while he himself though it his duty to tell the British public the real truth about China at the time. They became involved with the British China Friendship Association, Derek taking on the secretaryship of the Cambridge branch. He spent rather more time on this than on his studies. Hongying could not settle as long as he wasn't doing what she felt to be a fruitful occupation. In addition, the Cambridgeshire climate of damp and cold was making her ill again.

They moved back to London once more, zealously telling anyone interested about the New China. Derek found part time work on a magazine, Far East Trade, and gave lessons on Chinese. He also taught for the Workers Educational Association and the Cambridge Extra Mural Board. But the British China friendship Association still absorbed most of their energies, travelling throughout the country giving talks. Hongying taught Finchley Quakers to eat with chopsticks out of porcelain bowls.

On a 1959 visit to China, Hongying noted tremendous progress since the country's liberation. She noted industrial improvement, albeit through

Soviet involvement. They experienced a feeling of ease amongst the people, liberation, self confidence, which she hadn't known while living there before. Women were freeing themselves from household chores and unrelieved childminding. She wanted to visit her family in Changting but this was not yet open to foreigners. She went alone with Derek staying behind in Beijing.

They travelled back to Britain by the Trans Siberian Railway, enjoying a stopover in Leningrad as guests of Russian Friends. Hongying became fascinated by Russia and thought the language beautiful: "Language is the key to understanding of a people…." She kept up a correspondence with one of their hosts for years, even learnt Russian herself.

Derek began to teach Chinese at Holborn College later to become the Central London Polytechnic. Later, Hongying joined him as they both taught Modern Chinese. Derek was in charge of the Chinese section while Hongying taught Chinese Literature. Alongside this work was their continuous political writing and organising the China Political Study group. Hongying "had a wonderfully clear mind and expressed her ideas with logic and directness in plain language that all could understand… As always she was the educator…."

Another friend recalls that Hongying "was a splendid hostess, did us proud with excellent eats to help out our endless discussions… great warmth of manner, endlessly generous with money for whatever was needed. If you were upset she would make time to listen and help…" Usually her clothing was plain and unadorned but when she attended functions like those at the Chinese Embassy she wore lovely silk dresses and jackets.

Derek was now general secretary of the British Chinese Friendship Association. By 1966 the Chinese revolution was gathering momentum. Staff at the Chinese Embassy in London battled on the streets with the police and the British Embassy in Beijing was burnt to the ground. Support for China decreased and there was whole scale desertion of the Chinese cause by people in general.

On the couple's 1975 visit to China, Derek was allowed to accompany Hongying to the family home in Changting though they had to stay in the official guest house. At this time a photograph shows about fifty members of her family gathered together. Ten years later in a similar picture, the only member of Hongying's generation was her eldest sister in law, Da-Sao, now an old woman of 88 who didn't recognise anyone else.

English began to be in demand and the couple were now invited to go to China for six months at a time to teach at Fuzhou and Xiamen. This was much more satisfactory for Hongying though she did complain at times that they were treated like tourists and not allowed to talk to the peasants.

廖鴻英
LIAO HONGYING
BRYAN
BORN 24 DECEMBER 1905
DIED 21 FEBRUARY 1998
ALSO
H. DEREK
BRYAN
BORN 16 DECEMBER 1910
DIED 17 SEPTEMBER 2003

She met her old teacher, Lui Cifu aged 84. "You were my favourite pupil..." Officials kept close watch on Derek and Hongying making it difficult to talk intimately with her own family. From 1979 to 1985, they went back to China every year for several months, mostly teaching. Once retired they were received as honoured guests.

By the late 1980s they decided to leave London now wanting a quiet life. Hongying was decreasingly sharp, her sight and hearing failing a little and was happy to end her days in what she described as a place with history. They bought a house in Norwich where Hongying came to love her garden, treating her roses like the teacher she was. She cut them back hard and trained them for their own good! Work for China decreased but in 1989 the Tiananmen massacre broke Hongying's spirit. She cried for many days. Activities with Quakers increased and Derek finally came into membership too even becoming co-Clerk of the Meeting. They made a home for a succession of Chinese students and Scholars making up in a small way for the lack of their own children.

We record with sadness the death of our friend Liao Hongying who died peacefully at home on Saturday February 21st 1998. The funeral was held after the manner of Friends with burial in the Gildencroft on Thursday 26th 1998. A large group of family and Ffriends attended the Meeting for Funeral afterwards. We give thanks for her heroic life.

February 21 1998

E

The Eddington Family

The Eddington dynasty (for that is what it felt like to all of us who knew and respected them) benefitted Norfolk Quakers for well over a century. It has also been said that Eddington men all married strong women!

Alexander Eddington was born into a Quaker family in Congresbury, Somerset and educated at Didcot Friends School. He came to Norwich to join in partnership with Henry Brown in 1869, successfully trading as tea and coffee dealers on Gentlemans Walk facing the marketplace. Brown was Clerk to Norwich Meeting for a good number of years. Alexander quickly became absorbed into the life and work of the Quaker Meeting here. His first recorded task appeared:

> *in consequence of the decease of David Ballans who had copied the minutes of the Monthly Meeting, Alexander Eddington has expressed a willingness to undertake it in future on the same terms viz 50/- per annum and is therefore appointed...*

He married his first wife Maria, his partner's niece, in September 1871 and together they built up a prominent role within the Society. Alexander, for instance, visited applicants for membership, became a Trustee, represented Norwich at Quarterly Meeting, was on Yearly Charge Committee and on Ministry and Oversight Committee.

By March 1876 the minutes record Eddington feeling "it to be his duty to hold Meetings with the public in a few places..." and the Meeting encouraged him "to proceed with the work to which [they] believed he [was] called, trusting alone in the Lord for strength and guidance...".

By March the following year it was:

> *the judgement of the meeting that the time is come when Henry*

Brown may be released from the office of Clerk and that Alexander Eddington be requested to fill that position...

Alexander, modest to a fault, wasn't sure. However he continued to represent Norwich at Quarterly Meeting, was appointed auditor and given leave to examine the lists of members. In December he signed his first recorded minute "A.E. Clerk this time."

Maria died in 1878.

Alexander and his second wife, Florence, became stalwarts of the Meeting, their influences reaching far and wide. He became known for his "... wise and timely help, quietly given and much valued." This was the time of great national education reform with elementary schools being made compulsory. It was the parents of these children that the act benefitted that came to benefit themselves from the Adult and First Day School Movement. The Eddingtons, with their joint vision and foresight, embraced this movement and quickly began classes born out of the Sunday Scripture Reading classes both at Goat Lane and the Gildencroft.

To meet a need of the populace at large, as he saw it, Eddington widened his evangelical ministry, holding gatherings in public places, engaging speakers and gospellers to visit at the Gildencroft. Services misnamed Mission Meetings were established with prepared addresses and hymnsinging. The Adult Schools Movement produced a hymnbook for these

A group of Friends photographed in he 1890's organising the first fundraising sale for the Meeting. Manthorpe is on the far left of the first row, The Eddingtons are centre second row.

Meetings "with sufficient variety... adapted to the many occasions which occur for thanksgiving...".

The scope of spiritual provision widened with Bible meetings and Mothers' Meetings. There was opposition in certain quarters on the grounds that teaching people to read on the Sabbath increased secularisation and teaching writing to the poor might prove a big incentive to forgery. Meals were prepared by a team of women Friends led by Florence and served before classes began on First Day mornings at tables set with specially commissioned crested china. Financial records declare payment of a final invoice for tableware sufficient for 700 sittings. Whilst this was a social or economic necessity for some students, Eddington maintained it was a bonding time, an expression of belonging. It nevertheless brought suggestions of Eucharistic leanings.

Alexander Eddington and Joseph Rowntree together read a paper at the First Day Schools Conference announcing estimates in 1894 that there were 213 admissions to the Society of Friends nationally by convincement through the Adult Schools.

Alexander and Florence's son Arthur joined his father in the grocery business and in his parents work within the Society of Friends. Together they set up a network of Coffee Carts across the city, aimed at the cattle drovers bringing stock to market in the centre.

Arthur and his wife Doris became Weighty Friends within the Society, continuing the Schools work, continuing oversight of (I have heard it expressed) "pretty much everything." It was well known that he was passionately interested in the history of Quakers both locally and nationally so was approached in the early 1930s by Quintin Gurney, a descendent of the family of 19th century bankers and textile importers. There was a collection of Gurney family papers that might be made available to the Society of Friends. Eddington negotiated between Gurney and the Library of the Society in London but not before he (Eddington) took laborious copies for his own use. Legend prevails that he might have used a secretary but if so it becomes unclear who authorised the omissions.

The originals were eventually purchased for Friends House Library but not, as is the inevitable Quaker custom, without protracted correspondence and minute making. Were the papers to be insured? Was this really necessary? Who would take responsibility?

"Gurney to Nickalls (the librarian in London at the time). Barclays Bank Ltd, Bank Plain, Norwich... First of all I do not think it necessary to insure against the loss of the MSS as you so kindly say that you will give an undertaking to exercise all proper care in its custody and use and you may look upon this as a letter of indemnity. As regards the copyright I am quite

MARY IRENE
EDDINGTON
DIED 22ND NOV. 1996,
AGED 68 YEARS.
ANTHONY BRIAN
EDDINGTON
DIED 1ST FEB. 2007
AGED 83

willing that you should have freedom in this matter as I feel confident that you will use it with discretion… I hope you will let Mr Eddington have every access to the collection, and if he should wish to take some of the letters away temporarily I hope you will accede to his request on his giving you a written acknowledgement that they are in his possession…"

Mr Quintin Gurney has deposited in the library four hundred and twenty five letter to and from members of the Gurney family and its connections including 56 letters of Elizabeth Fry, 84 letters of Amelia Opie, 22 of Joseph Gurney Bevan, 9 of William Wilberforce, 2 important letters of Joseph Sturge and 31 of members of the Buxton family containing many references to the Anti Slavery campaign.

On behalf of the Society of Friends we accept with gratitude this loan which makes an important addition to the resources available in the library. We propose that it should be known as the Gurney MSS.

A letter dated 6th May 1931 which is attached has been received from Mr Gurney indemnifying the Society in regard to the MSS provided the conditions as to their custody set out in the librarian's letter of 28th March 1931 to Arthur Eddington are observed…..We are glad to accept these conditions and we also thank Mr Gurney for the freedom which he accords us in the matter of the use and publication of the MSS.

We cordially agree to his suggestion for the temporary loan to Arthur Eddington of any MSS which he may wish to borrow from this collection. The letters are accompanied by a detailed catalogue and précis compiled by Arthur Eddington to whom we accord our warm thanks for this careful and very serviceable piece of work….."

Minute 4: meeting of the Library Committee 3/11/1931

We have included extracts from this correspondence to emphasise the integrity of the sources themselves, the anxiety of all parties to be seen to value the sources and the patience of Eddington – or his secretary - in those pre photocopier days.

In 1945 at the close of World War 2 Eddington may have offered some of his own researches and copies of documents to the library. There is a separate letter dated November 14th 1945 and held with the Gurney correspondence copies at Norwich which illustrates the conditions under which all conscientious librarians are constrained. Eddington's personal integrity would not allow himself to do otherwise.

The library has reached a stage where it can no longer house all of the books and to allow for the return of those displaced and purchased during the last six years we have taken out about 1000 absolute duplicates which Meetings for Sufferings agrees may be placed wherever suitable.....the difficulty is that there is only two of us to do it all.

This last explains why there is still this cache of papers at Goat Lane, Arthur Eddington's legacy in effect[1]. It is these copies that provide the sources for some of these chapters. He writes:

I can only hope that these few extracts may convey a slight impression of the treasures contained in the collection of manuscripts that has been placed in the care of the Society through the kindness of Mr Quintin Gurney. I know that he is keenly desirous that they may be made more readily accessible to any who can make use of them

Arthur and Doris had one son, John, of their own and adopted another, Anthony. Anthony and his wife Mary also led an active life within and on behalf of the Society of Friends. Anthony became a lecturer in Animal Husbandry at Easton College whilst also clerking the Meeting. They were great stalwarts and supporters of Quaker Worship in the new estate of Bowthorpe in the western outskirts of Norwich. Alexander and Florence (and Maria), Arthur, Doris, John and Mary Eddington have graves in the Gildencroft. Anthony moved to live with his son, John, in Lancashire after Mary's death but his ashes were placed upon her grave.

1 We have treated them as a secondary source as Eddington spent a great deal of time editing them.

The Forster Family

From The Testimony to the Grace of God as shown in the Life of William Forster. March 1855.

> *...He was the 2nd son of William and Elizabeth Forster born on 23rd March 1784. His parents were committed members of the Religious Society of Friends and anxiously concerned that their children might grow up with severance for the Blessed Truths of the Gospel of Christ and with a value for all the testimonies and practices which we believe flow from that Heavenly Source. Our dear Friend was from his childhood of a very kind and affectionate disposition. When very young he shewed much tender feeling for the sorrow and troubles of others and would seek by acts of kindness and self sacrifice to alleviate the pain and sickness which he saw around him... In his youth he was greatly affected by the cruelties inflicted on the slave...*
>
> *...His father had designed to introduce him into his own business, that of a Local Land Agent, and was training him for that occupation...*

In the spring of 1815, just as the wars with France were drawing to a close, William married Anna Buxton, daughter of Thomas Fowell Buxton. Buxton himself became known for his tireless work in opposition to the iniquitous trade in African slaves and has a Blue Plaque to his memory on the front of Goat Lane Meeting House. The couple settled firstly in Bridport, Dorset. They were delighted at the birth of an infant son.

From The Testimony again "but as it became evident that Impressions of Religious Duty were requiring of him a larger sacrifice of time and energy..." William left them both for five years travelling at home and abroad in the ministry:

...visit[ing] nearly every Meeting of The Society of Friends on this island...

...In 1837 the family moved back to Norwich and for some years after his coming amongst us he travelled with our full concurrence in difficult parts of the Kingdom in the exercise of his gift in the Ministry... In the spring of 1843 he felt compelled to Travel in The Ministry [once again], to Ireland specially seeking younger Friends...

...The continuance of the African Slave Trade with all its attendant cruelties... often brought him into painful exercise of mind ...

The Testimony to the Grace of God as shown in the Life of William Forster.
March 1855.

The Testimony continues at some length, many many pages copied out in laborious handwriting in the Minute Book. It took some months to agree upon the wording with the Committee appointed to research and compile it coming back to each Business Meeting and asking for further time to continue. No man could be disappointed with their finished work on his behalf.

In brief, William accompanied by some friends, fellow Friends, went to America taking their evangelistic Quakerism to what were then termed as The Slave States. The Minutes record William's fate on that journey.

A letter from William Holmes... being one of the deputation to accompany our beloved Friend as his companion in this service...

"It will be pretty generally known to Friends that he had entered very little upon the religious engagement set forth in the Certificates granted him by his Monthly and Quarterly Meetings; in the course of our travel on the mission to which we were appointed by the Yearly Meeting, more particularly in the early parts of it, we were amongst Friends and attended Meetings at Mount Pleasant, Cincinnatti, Richmond and Bloomfield in Indianna in all which our dear Friend laboured very acceptably in the Cause of his Divine Master. When at Madison in Wisconsin he felt his mind drawn to the inhabitants of the place a public meeting was appointed. It was not largely attended but proved a quiet season and he was enabled to deliver the Gospel message to the relief as, I believe, of his mind.

At St Louis our little band became acquainted with several who had been members of our Society; they gladly availed themselves of the opportunity of sitting down with us on First Day at our hotel. Dear W.F. was again very acceptably engaged both in testimony and supplication and after this proceeded to the south and having accomplished visits to most of the Governers of the Slave States, our dear Friend's mind seemed renewedly drawn to the Meetings of Friends in Eastern Tenessee. These were part of those alluded to in his Certificate as surrounded by a slave population. On the seventh day, the 31st of December we reached Hickery Valley where a few friends reside. There were nearly 50 in attendance at a Meeting on 1st Day morning.

On 2nd Day we proceeded to Friendsville near which is Newberry Meeting House where a Meeting had been appointed at his request. It was attended by about 200 persons, mostly Friends. He was much favoured in both these Meetings, in the last particularly his communication was very impressive. The Friends of that Meeting in speaking of it afterwards said it was strikingly applicable to their State and believed that his service among them had been blessed.

On the 3rd Day we set out for Lost Creek Meeting, distance about 40 miles, and proceeded about 10 miles to a Ferry House on the Holston River where we lodged. Next morning our dear Friend felt very unwell, but desirous of continuing the journey. We set out but had proceeded only a few hundred yards when it became evident that it was not safe to proceed. He was therefore got back to the house we had left and where he peacefully breathed his last after an illness of little more than three weeks..."

The illness is thought to have been pneumonia. On the 27th of 1st Month 1854 William was buried in Tennessee, North America.

Anna died on the 5th June 1855, "a minister 42 years".

It is remarked by those who well knew her that altho[sic] living in what would be called the gay world, and partaking to a certain extent in its transitory pleasures, she was evidently not of it. She much valued being with her Aunt Rachel Gurney at Keswick in Norfolk. In her she found a sympathising and judicious friend; and here many of her associates being seriously disposed her character shewed [sic] itself...

As a girl she wrote to her mother 1806:

I have been brought to strive with myself and to a very great increased desire to forsake the evil and cleave to the good, and it seems to me that I am being led for I feel that my earnest prayers to know my heart are in some measure answered by the humiliation I feel... It is very hard to overcome those sins which do most easily beset me...

On one occasion in particular beside the grave of her youngest brother, a Midshipman in the navy, who died in Haslar Hospital at Gosport and was buried in the cemetery there, her voice was heard after the customary service had been performed; and it is well known that when Eliz. Fry first visited the female prisoners in Newgate, Anna Buxton was her only companion.

She [Anna] had the company of her loved friend Pricilla Gurney and in1817 united with her in a general visit to Friends in Ireland...

She wrote of those travels, that the union with Pricilla was "strengthening and comforting to us both..." and of :

being restored with a relieved mind to my beloved husband in comfortable habitation makes me ready afresh to say 'Oh that we may praise the Lord for his goodness'...

...She was a woman of good judgement, deeply instructed in the things of Christ and greatly interested in the welfare of our Religious Society....her faith was often brought to a severe test in having to give up her husband for services [overseas]...Deeply did she enter into exercise and sympathy with him in all such engagements...She undoubtedly believed [in] the Divine Will in these trying desperations.....

...The extreme tenderness for animals which she evinced at all periods of her life was not merely a feeling of love and admiration but one of deep conviction that there was a happy place in the creation assigned to them and that for man to treat them with cruelty was absolutely sinful. This produced a willingness to undergo mental suffering on their account and a readiness on all occasions to plead their cause; which in more than one instance she felt constrained to do with those who had the care of public menageries.... [and was concerned about] the hardening effect which an indulgence in such cruelty had in the minds of those who practised it...

[She had] a tender feeling of compassion for the oppressed African Race...preferring disuse of the produce of slave labour as far as was practicable...engaging in the arduous efforts which they made to obtain freedom for the slaves....

Nursed by her beloved sister in law who had been her companion for some months:

a rapid sinking was apparent. A ...holy cheerfulness marked her last hours and supported by her tenderly loved son she peacefully and gently passed away...

The collection of eighteenth and nineteenth century Testimonies held within our Minute Books seem to be an indication of a lost world, a language and sentiment long abandoned.

Their son, also William, the infant left behind whilst his parents Travelled in the Ministry, was the instigator of the 1870 Education Reform Act. Only Anna Forster remained in Norwich to be buried in the Gildencroft.

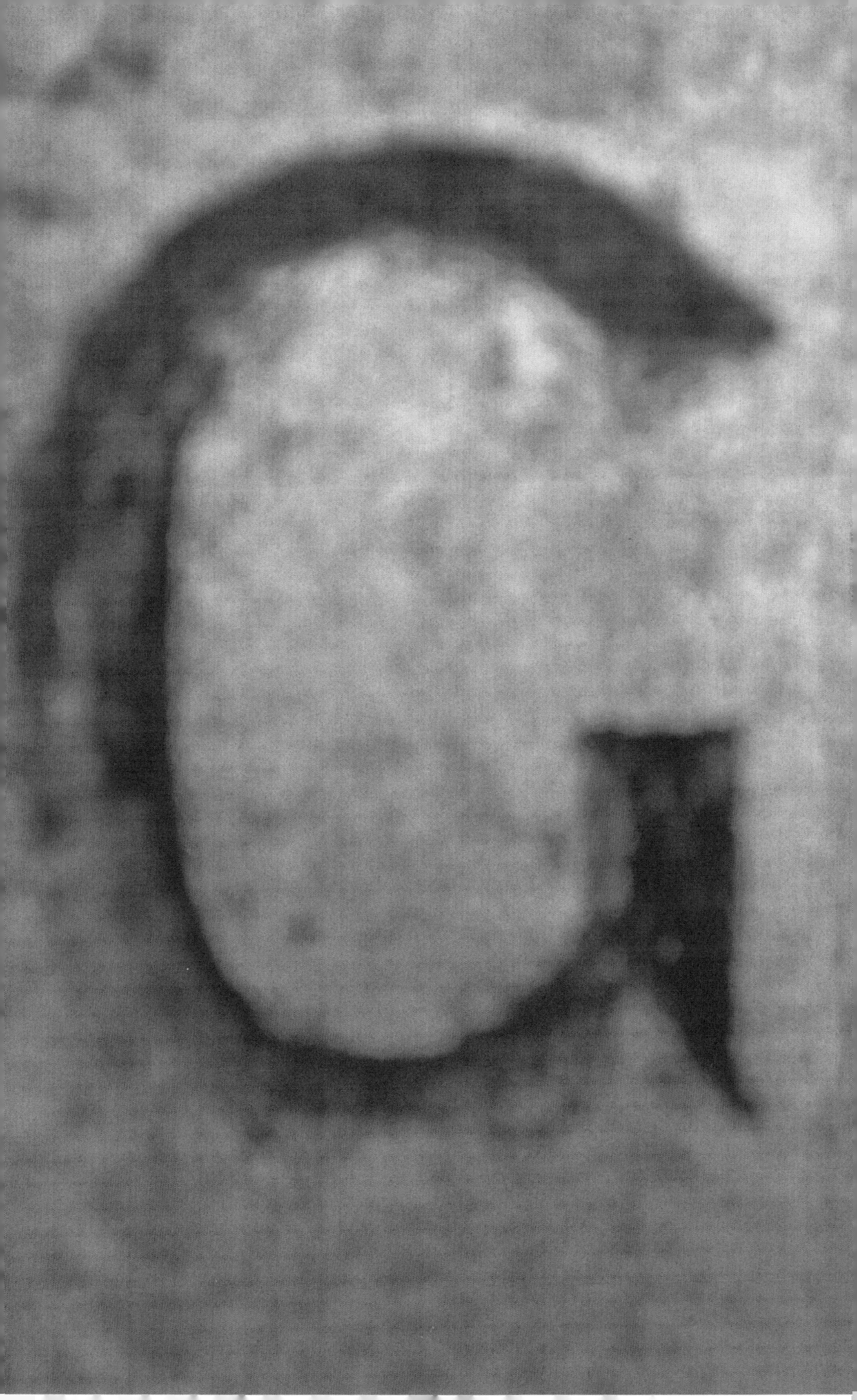
G

Gravemakers and Headstones

Although right from the start of interments the position of each burial was drawn on a map and recorded in the ledgers, most graves in the Gildencroft were unmarked for a century and a half. The first formal request for a stone had been in 1692 when "the sense of the Meeting [is] wholly against it and that for the future, no one be permitted to set up any". The Minute continues asking that Friends "should continue to persuade those who have set up any to remove them".[1]

... Although this Meeting does not approve the erecting of any Monuments over ye Graves of ye deceased, yet whereas some person or persons have privately without any order or advise of our Monthly Meeting, taken away some posts or marks at graves, this Meeting Does conclude of a disorderly practice and ye practicers disorderly therein...

Norwich Monthly Meeting 9th mo 1711

Minute advising removal of existing gravestones in 1717:

This meeting being informed that Friends in places have gone to the vain and empty custom of erecting monuments over the dead bodies of Friends by Stones, Inscriptions, Tombstones, Etc. And being very desirous Friends should keep to a commendable plainness and simplicity in this as well as other respects it is therefore the advice of this Meeting that all such monuments as are already in place over dead bodies of Friends should be removed as much as may be with discretion and conveniency; and that none be any when made or set up by or over the dead bodies of Friends or others in Friends' Burial Places for time to come.

Norwich Monlthy Meeting 1717

1 N.R.O. SF54.

There are Minutes reporting dealings with Ann Byar, the widow of James, an early wealthy Quaker. Byar's will stipulated that his widow should arrange a very flamboyant and grandiose funeral in his honour. The cortege was to have an inordinate number of plumed horses to convey his coffin through the streets of Norwich and a sum of money was left so that several poor but deserving Quaker children should act as Dumb Mutes in the procession. Having carried out her late husband's wishes and with him safely interred in the Gildencroft, Ann then proceeded to erect an ornate memorial table edifice of immense proportions on his grave.

Four Friends, Richard Kett, Richard White, John Parker and John Gurney Junior were desired to go to the Widow Byar "and entreat of her to remove ye Tomb that is over her husband's Grave in Friends Burial Ground". The Meeting's Elders spent the next few years in protracted negotiations with her to have the stone removed. In 1720 there is reference to the fact that as she "... now shared the same stone..." the correspondence must be at an end. There is a distinct air of resignation in the Clerk's final minute.

Norwich Meeting continued to direct that all remaining stones should be removed and encouraged any steps to do so.

> *"As plainness and Simplicity is not only becoming but agreeable to the Profession we make to the World, so this Meeting having soundly considered the great number of Gravestones erected in our Burial ground and the inconsistency that appears thereby it is very desirous to have the same removed..."*
>
> Norwich Monthly Meeting 3rd Month 1757

After yet a further decade Friends were "not without hopes that the very few yet remaining may in time be removed..."

At the same time as they were dealing with what felt to them an embarrassment with the memorials, Quakers record having to consider two ongoing troubles in the Burial Gound. Friends arrived for Worship on horseback or by horse drawn carriage. Meetings for Worship often lasted for some hours and the animals needed shelter and fodder, and the grassed areas were becoming neglected by those Friends who were supposed to keep it tidy.

In 1717 or 18 it was decided "to erect a stable... to look after publick Friends horses...". Sixty-three Friends together raised £102 12/- for the cost of the build. The Meeting agreed:

> *... ye Thomas Paine should take 2/20d per week for Hay for their horses yt stand in ye stable in our burying ground, they yt give their*

Horses no oats should pay 2/6d per week... And that no person do presume to put any horses into ye Burial Ground without the leave of this Meeting...

The horses were a mixed blessing as although they went a great way to keeping the grass down they also trampled the graves.

... so no horses be allowed to feed therein [ie the area that had graves] and the Gildencroft be kept in a decent and becoming order... [Horses] that may want grass may be turned without detriment to the Ground

It was minuted on 8th 8mo 1731 that an Edward Fenn could

... have liberty to make Ropes in the Burying Ground not doing any damage to ye graves...

Norwich Monthly Meeting 8th Month 1731

In 1752 they dealt with yet more livestock problems when it was ordered "... that no fowls shall be kept to incommode the Stable..." and the number of horses left were getting out of hand. Friends could have "the use of the Burial Ground for One horse" or if you were a member of the Gurney family "Henry Gurney not to exceed two at one time". Then there was the cattle grazing; at a Meeting on 30th 9mo 1774 there were

some objections made to the feeding on our Burial Ground with cattle... It be fed with Horses only in future.

Norwich Monthly Meeting 9th Month 1774

By 1773 the stable was in serious disrepair despite Friends "having it screwed up with some strong planks". The decision was finally made to take down what was left of the building and "to make out a Driving-way to the Great Meeting House" and to use money left in the Langwade Gift to repair the wall and "take the needful care to have any part of it moved when necessary...."

Meetings for Worship for Burials in the Gildencroft, in The Manner of Friends were dignified affairs. Richenda Cunningham, nee Gurney, writes to her sister Louisa Hoare having attended the burial of their Aunt Rachel, wife of Richard and mother of Richard junior...

On Thursday morning we all assembled at that solemn Gildencroft.

I felt a good deal in our all being assembled there once again, as well as the loss of our dear Aunt. The sight of dear Anna, dragged in her chair by her old servants, with Richard at her side, following the coffin was truly affecting. Joseph knelt by the grave and prayed impressively and beautifully and Betsy [Elizabeth Fry] also gave an encouraging address dwelling on the joy and peace which attend the death of the righteous. The Meeting was crowded by a very mixed multitude. I thought the Ministry beautiful and most edifying...

Richenda Cunningham

The burial of John Joseph Gurney is described by his daughter Anna...

The funeral was wonderfully interesting as a spectacle. The crowded roads, the mourning city, would have been most touching in any case; but that very sort of interest took off a little, to my feelings, from the settled solemnity of the day, except at the grave, where the silence was as peaceful as it was awful and profound...

Anna Gurney

The Burial Register[2] is a grubby little volume, obviously much used and thumbed, even though the hand that has made the entries is clear and even. My suspicion is that, although the gravemaker has the keeping of this book it is not he who makes the entries.

John Stone

John Stone was the 'grave maker' from start of this register. It was his responsibility to dig, record the graves dug and where. He records two graves on each page, the wording is by and large the same and he makes no comment upon nor distinction between a grave for rich or poor, twenty stone man or stillborn infant, except to record if the grave has been brick lined. Few such linings are recorded; as well as time and labour it would have involved extra expense and the grave space would not be available after the usual hundred years for redigging. Stone's only written comment upon completion of a grave was in the case of Thomas Aggs...

...GENTLEMAN [who] died at the Goat Lane Meeting instantaneously at the Meeting of Discipline.

One has to wonder why. Was he mourning the demise of Aggs, a spe-

2 N.R.O. SF113.

cial Friend or remarking that he perhaps got what was coming to him? Struck down by The Lord!?

John Stone's last grave, his 98th in the Gildencroft before handing over the task to Isaac Harrison of Quaker Lane was to make the grave for two week old Anna Bidwell (see above) in August 1830.

The very next entry is for Stone's own grave in October 1830. Harrison records that Stone was aged about 43 of St Clements Parish and a weaver.

Issac Harrison

Harrison dug Martha and Spicer Crowe's graves. He had the sad task of preparing a grave in 1847 for his own sixteen year old daughter Christianna. He also seems to have dug his own wife, Mary's, grave in March 1860. He records her age there as 67 so he must have been a good age himself at the time, a good age to be digging six feet down through varying soils in all weathers. He makes no mention of either relationship in his records; the wording of all his entries does not vary.

The next but one grave he prepared after Mary's was for the last member of the Gurney family to be buried in the Gildencroft - that of Joseph John. Gurney's grave is brick lined.

Norwich Quakers weren't the only Meeting seeking standardisation of their headstones. And taking a very long time to discern the way forward! Meetings in comparable cities such as Liverpool and Bristol sought Bidwell's thoughts on the matter.

In the mid nineteenth century, Bidwell, as clerk in Norwich replied to the clerk at Liverpool

> *With regard to my own ideas on the subject [of securing uniformity] I think with Thee that where Monthly Meetings can come to a united conclusion to raise a special fund for the care of the Burial Ground including the appearance of the gravestones, that would be the better course, a small standing committee having the matter under its care...*
>
> Bidwell [NRO SF376/2]

Brown received a letter from George Thomas, clerk at Bristol 14th October 1850 [NRO SF376/4] containing a long list of queries which Bidwell patiently answered. Bidwell was a conscientious clerk keeping drafts of all his outgoing correspondence so we are able to follow his thoughts... even if they are scribbled on a small scrap of paper.

Thomas – Size?

Bidwell – 12 inches square and 4 inches thick.
Thomas –What inscribed on them?
Bidwell – Initials of the deceased.
Thomas – Chiselled or painted black?
Bidwell – Chiselled.
Thomas –Map or register? Cost?"
Bidwell – Stones bought in lots of about 50 to 100 at a cost of 7/9d each and the letters cost 3d each for cutting and are about 2 ¼ inches in length.
Thomas – Expense defrayed?
Bidwell – By M.M.
Thomas – Committee? To regulate?
Bidwell – Yes.
Thomas – Not in membership?
Bidwell – No difference.

Bidwell has preserved a quotation[3] from Joseph Stanley, a stonemason, who recommends

> *four inch thick Portland stone [and offers] to supply stones 1 foot 8 inches by 2 feet by 3 inches at seven shillings with lettering at 1d per letter and others slightly larger at a price of 10/- or 9/- if there is a quantity...*
>
> Joseph Stanley, stonemason

Practices were finally agreed and adopted universally in the second half of the nineteenth century[4] and recorded by the local Meetings thus....

> *Regulations adopted by Norwich Monthly Meeting in regard to gravestones in the Burial Ground in Norwich. 1st. That in all future interments in this burial ground the surviving relatives or other representatives of the deceased may require to have a stone laid down with an inscription in accordance with the Yearly Meeting's Minute: and in case the deceased was in membership that the expense be defrayed out of a special subscription to be raised under the direction of the Monthly Meeting.*
>
> *2nd. That the surviving relatives of other representatives of persons who have been interred in the Burial ground previous to the date of these regulations to be allowed to have such stones placed over existing*

3 N.R.O. SF376/14
4 N.R.O. SF266

graves; but that in all such cases, the expense to be defrayed by the person requiring them.

3rd. That the stone to be laid down be 2feet 6inches long by 2feet wide and three inches thick.; or for children under 10 years, 2feet long by 1foot 6 inches wide; and that the material be Portland Stone: the inscription to be simply chiselled and not painted; the name to be in what are termed Blockletters, the age and date in figures.

4th. That each stone be placed in the centre of the grave, at an equal distance from the head and foot and if a second stone be required to be placed over the same grave in consequence of a second interment therein, that it be placed close to the former ones taking care to observe the same proportionate distance from the head and the foot.

5th. That the surface of the stones be placed level with the ground and that care be taken to prevent them sinking below it.

6th. That a standing committee be appointed to carry out these regulations to provide the stones and to have the care of the Burial ground generally.

Norwich Monthly Meeting 12th Month 1851

Norwich Record Office SF67's assorted loose minutes outlines other responsibilities of this new Committee thus:

To verify digest of births marriages and deaths.

To examine map of burial ground to see that position of all new graves has been entered in the minute book.

Every fourth year appoint committee to see by actual measurement that all graves since last appointment have been correctly marked on the map

Harrison dug Amelia Opie's bricklined grave and that of her father, the surgeon John Alderson, in the farthest left hand corner of the burial ground. He prepared at least 125 graves in the Gildencroft. An appointed Friend held the key to the burial ground and he would have to go to them to gain access. He was not allowed to charge the bereaved family any more than 1/- for the task but "may be permitted to accept more if they offered it..."

The order for Harrison's own burial is signed by Henry Brown and took place "on 19th 8th month 1869 at half past ten o clock in the forenoon" By now the records were kept on burial slips pasted into the record book, but still two to a page. Harrison's is the thirteenth grave on the new record slip system and sadly it does not record who did him the honour of digging his grave.

Employment prospects were changing within the Meeting "rendered vacant by the decease of Isaac Harrison".

To Robert and Catherine Murphy. We are willing to engage your services for the care of this Meeting House in Norwich [Goat Lane]. It is an agreement involving as I think I named to you in London- keeping the premises clean, lighting fires whenever required for the Meetings and other purposes of Friends, being in attendance when Meetings are held and waiting upon friends if required on the premises. It is also intended to arrange for Robert Murphy to have charge of the Friends Burial Ground which is situated about half a mile from the Meeting House. The duties of this appointment involve the cutting of the grass sufficiently, trimming the raised mounds over graves, cleaning the gravestones and keeping the paths rolled and free from weeds etc. In connection with it there would be to have graves dug when required, to make certain arrangements for funerals and take some superintendence of them. The gravedigging is of course a special charge at rates fixed by Friends. Accommodation found free of rent, free coals, 17/- per week. Find own brushes and cleaning stuffs...

SF285/12/4. 1872

To W.H. and M.E. Pickering... W.H.P will be required to keep the graves in the B.G. sufficiently mown and to trim the grass over the raised mounds and around the stones; to roll the paths and keep them free from weeds and otherwise to keep the ground neat and clean. W.H.P will also be required to make certain arrangements for funerals and to take some superintendence of them. Also to order and superintend the digging of graves... 20/- subsistence plus coals... 19/-?

Draft letter 17.6.1869

Mr and Mrs Pickering have graves in the Gildencroft, and soon "S. Croome and his wife" are caretakers at Goat Lane and there is no longer any mention of duties concerning the Gildencroft.

After the Minutes concerning the standardisation of memorial stones were recorded, a committee was appointed consisting of the usual names of Weighty Friends of the time, Forster, Candler a miller from Cringleford, Bidwell, Goose (the main contractor for the rebuilding of Goat Lane in 1826) with Henry Brown as Clerk and Treasurer. There were applications for 37 stones to be put in place. An adult gravestone then cost an average of 13 shillings with ten for a child.

Twenty of these applications were for graves of direct line Gurneys still carrying the surname and about half as many again who had Gurney connections.

Emma Pearce nee Gurney wrote to Brown-

My dear Henry, I very much like the idea of my dear father's grave and the rest of our family being marked by the date and name. I suppose the records of the Meeting will give Thee the proper date... It is a pleasant memory and one I should much like. My father and mother were laid in one grave... Thy very affectionate, Emma Pearce nee Gurney.[5]

John Gurney wrote to Brown from his house in Hanover Terrace, Regents Park, London, NW on behalf of his brother, John Henry who, with his young son who has contracted measles, was staying with them...

J.H. Gurney thinks it very desirable that something should be done to put it [the burial ground] in a more satisfactory state and would be glad to have a list of the graves and an estimate for the cost of putting fresh upright stones. I also spoke to my sister, Mrs Ripley, who said she would like to visit the place. Perhaps Thou canst make an appointment to furnish her. Thine sincerely, J. Gurney.[6]

Samuel Gurney wrote to Henry Brown, October 25th 1881.

I have to thank Thee for Thy letter, also for the trouble Thou hast taken about the family gravestones. It is a good job done. I have carried out the same thing in our own burial ground at Barking where so many of my family rest. Next time I go to Norwich I should like to visit the Gildencroft and see what has been done...[7]

Thomas Aggs wrote to Brown, 22nd March 1882.

Hollywood, Clapham Common, London, SW.

Dear Friend, I hear from my relative Samuel Gurney that the gravestones of my ancestors are in a dilapidated state and require renovation. Will you kindly let me know who attends to this and what the

5 N.R.O. SF376/19

6 N.R.O. SF376/34

7 N.R.O. SF376/42

expenses will be. There are four that require attention...[8]

Samuel Gurney underwrote the cost of eleven gravestones. John Henry Gurney paid for three whilst Lucy Aggs nee Gurney paid for five. Not every friend was as willing. Thomas Aggs wrote to Brown. 6th May 1882. He has been insistent upon sorting out which grave holds which body!

The name of Thomas Aggs 1782 to which you refer in your letter was only an infant of a few months old and I do not think a stone necessary...[9]

Poor little scrap.

Henry Brown

Henry Brown was Clerk to Norwich Meeting for a staggering 38 years.

Norwich Monthly Meeting held 11th of 1st mo 1899... Minute 3. This meeting has expressed and desires to place on record its deep sense of the value of the services rendered by Henry Brown who occupied the position of Clerk for 38 years and in numberless other ways faithfully served the Monthly Meeting. We trust that for several years to come we shall have his presence with us and that he will be enabled to give his valuable help and advice to the Monthly Meeting.

Norwich Monthly Meeting 1st Month 1899[10]

Norwich Monthly Meeting 9th 5mo 1900. 39 present. Minute 1. A Burial Note has been brought in for Henry Brown of Norwich who died on the 24th day of 3rd mo 1900 aged 84 years and was buried in the Gildencroft Burial ground on the 29th day of the same. The death was registered at the Registry Office for West Wymer on the 26th day of 3mo 1900. We deeply feel the loss we have sustained by his removal and A. Eddington, F. Eddington, John Papps and William Newby are appointed to prepare a minute of testimony concerning him...

Norwich Monthly Mwwting 5th Month 1900

Norwich Monthly Meeting held at Yarmouth 14th 6mo 1900... Minute 2. Draft minute for H. Brown deceased... was of a very retiring

8 N.R.O. SF376/43

9 N.R.O. SF377/10

10 N.R.O. SF64

disposition... the last of a fraternity of men of fine character and although he never took so prominent a place in our Society as his brother Isaac of Ackworth and Kendal his influence was widely extended and most helpful to those around him... he was born in London, educated at Ackworth after which he lived 10 years in Brighton... in 1840, Brothers helped him take a small grocery business in Norwich... set the example of an honest persevering tradesman. We believe that throughout that time his first object was to do the will of his father in Heaven and to live with his conscience void of offence toward God and toward man... the minister who influenced his life more than any other was William Forster. [Brown] was very zealous in attending weekday and business meetings in various capacities besides being its Clerk for 38 years... never allowed his business to prevent his working for the good of his fellow men... Probably his own meeting was the place where above all others his influence for good was felt... By his removal we have lost a father and a pastor in one... On March 24 his sleep turned to unconsciousness and after lying in this state for about 12 hours he painlessly and peacefully entered upon his holy rest. Thus passed away at the ripe age of 84 one who for many years had faithfully served his generation and who had in a remarkable manner walked humbly with his God.

Norwich Monthly Meeting 6th Month 1900

Quakers firmly hold a testimony to equality. For every burial, of rich or poor, whether they are erected in a Quaker Burial ground or in a public cemetery, our stones, for we do now erect a memorial stone, continue to have the same simple wording and no memorial will be grander than another.

Today, each grave is contracted out by the Funeral Director arranging the individual interment. The work is now done with a mechanical digger and costs considerably more than Isaac Harrison's one shilling.

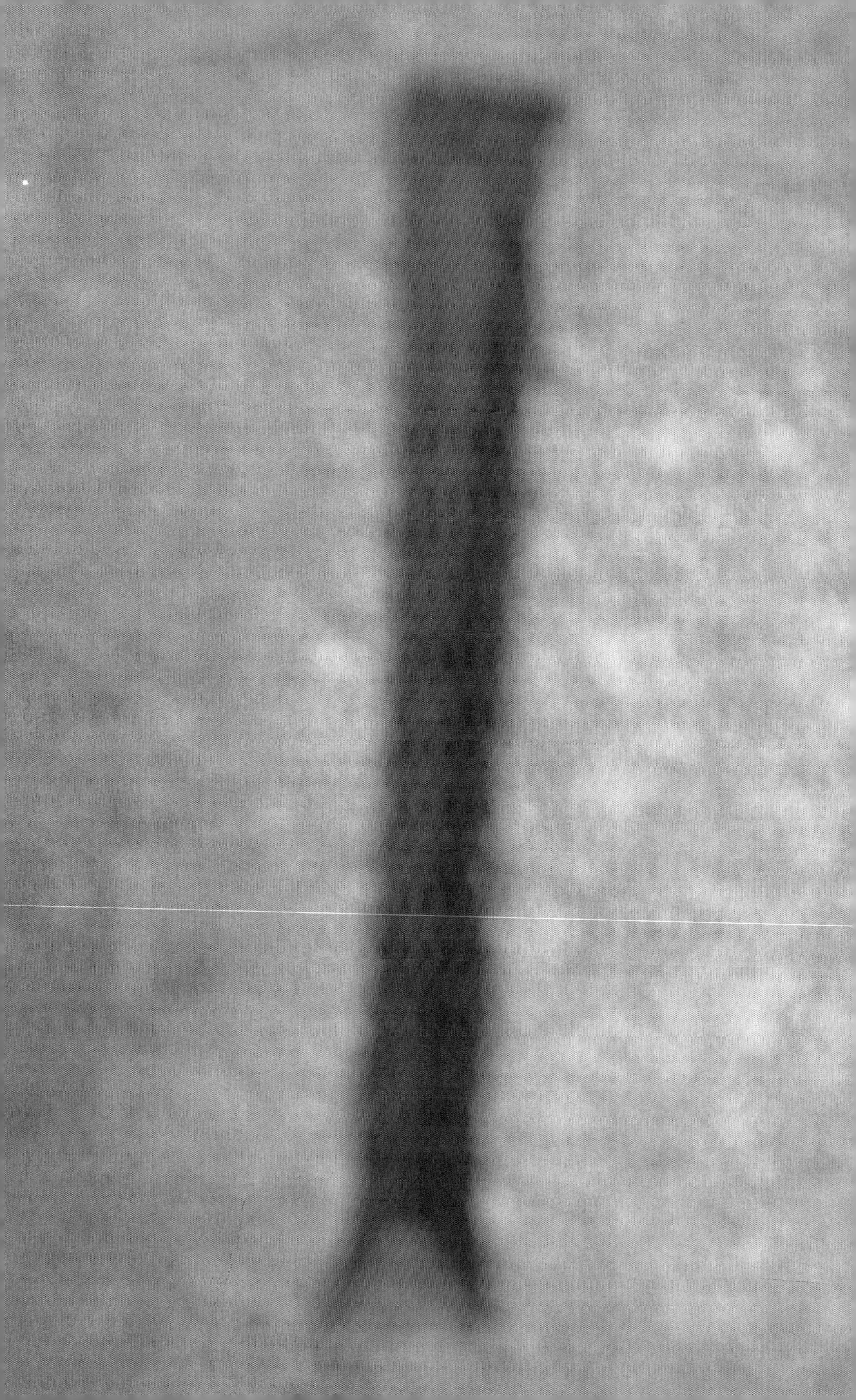

Infant Mortality

In 1690, when the Gildencroft was first opened as a burial ground for local Quakers the total population of Norwich was around 29,000. Two local studies (Edwards and Corfield) show that Norwich's death rates of 35.8 per thousand exceeded the national level.

By 1740 the rate was grudgingly down by point one per cent per thousand but children aged under ten years old accounted for nearly half the burials across the city at that time and infants alone for 45%. Look at the many tiny coffin shapes on the Gildencroft's burials map roll; it will break your heart. Epidemics, particularly of smallpox, were frequent and together with food shortages and high prices, the most vulnerable succumbed. It has already been shown that medical provision was sketchy.

Edwards conjects that any eighteenth and nineteenth century improvement in mortality statistics may have been due to some expansion of health facilities, inoculation against smallpox and improved financial relief for the poor. Penelope Corfield [using Bills of Mortality as her source material] argues that Norwich had inherited several housing and sanitation problems in the old city centre and was rapidly gaining new ones in the unplanned districts of growth beyond the city walls. She notes that in all but nine of the years 1707-50 burials across the city exceeded baptisms. I have to ask has she taken into account that fact that the Quaker infants buried in the Gildencroft are, of course, unbaptized. Although impressed by the efforts of the civil and medical authorities, she nevertheless describes the early nineteenth century city as crowded, smelly and insanitary.

After 1870 there was a definite reduction in general mortality. Fewer infants died in the 1880s but deaths rose again in the 1880s. As late as 1883, one quarter of the city's families depended upon wells for water, fewer than 5000 houses had a toilet. However, smallpox was recorded less often as a cause of death, the last outbreak being amongst prisoners in Norwich Castle. Typhus had been all but eradicated, and there were fewer incidences of typhoid, scarlet fever and tuberculosis.

Social class played little part in how many babies survived their birth and lived a healthy life. Joseph and Jane Gurney lost three children, Joseph, Mary and Henry. We have already seen the tragedies within the affluent Bidwell family. We should not forget tiny Thomas Aggs, who died aged less than a year old and who was considered unworthy of a headstone by his wealthy descendent of the same name.

Thomas and Rachel Hitchen lost four children; Thomas, aged one, Hannah aged five, another Hannah aged eighteen months - many families did this by calling the new child after the one who had died, and John who died aged only two.

The Lincoln family, Charles whose occupation is unrecorded and his wife Sarah, lost six children towards the close of the eighteenth century. Their daughter, Mary was eighteen weeks old when she died, their son Robert lived only two weeks. The following year they buried stillborn twins, the sex of whom is unrecorded. Three years later they lost another Mary at twelve weeks and four years later still Timothy died aged nine months. Sarah died aged only (by today's standards) 53 and is buried close to her children. Charles' grave seems to be elsewhere.

Isaac Harrison was a weaver when he wasn't required to dig graves. He and his wife Mary lost three children; Christopher born in 1831 lived to sixteen years but Lewis John, born in 1833 in a time of prevalent cholera, lived only six weeks. The following year there was another Lewis John who himself lived for only four years.

Every once in a while, Dear Friends, remember the sorrow of all these parents.

Jobs

The graves in the Gildencroft are of the richest of the rich to the poorest of the poor. The Gurney family are reputed to have enjoyed wealth second only to the Bank of England, and their Clerks and their Solicitors and the merchants with whom they did business while Mr Freare (d.1933) was, a poor general labourer at times living hand to mouth.

"Shoemaker" or "Cordwainer" might mean a single person in a lean-to banging away with a few nails and a bit of old hide or a manufacturer with any number of homeworkers and their work collected into extensive business premises. John Bousell (d.1801) was a leather cutter; John Siddell (d.1777) and Richard Meakins (d.1790] describe themselves as cordwainers while Thomas Rix (d.1782) was a shoemaker.

The textile industry worked in much the same way. The titles of the various trades involved in the production of a length of cloth are legion. Since the seventeenth century the Gurney firm had been known for their hand made cloth but late eighteenth century industrialisation was spreading down from the north of England. More and more huge mills churned our vast quantities of mass produced textiles. The new jacquard looms needed a greater height of space than the Norfolk home weavers could find and they could not compete with quantities of production. Several Norwich specialities were added to the Yorkshire repertoire and skilled operatives left the city to work in these mills. Norwich complained that these copies were cheap and nasty but nevertheless they were being snapped up with enthusiasm at home and abroad. Norfolk weavers who continued to struggle on alone creating shawls were paid by the number of hanks of yarn used, not by the day. There was no set average wage. 'Trucking' was used by unethical managers whereby vouchers for goods at shops owned by the firm were given instead of cash, or actual goods, whether useful to the weaver and his family or not, were given in lieu of payment. These had to be sold on for whatever they could get.

Joseph John Gurney [1888-1847], son of John and Caroline Gurney of Earlham Hall and brother of Elizabeth Fry, took their cause to heart and spent his Christmas of 1829 writing letters on behalf of the poor textile workers…

> *Almost total cessation of work is becoming very grievous... truly affecting to think of their sufferings in this cold weather… the uncertainty of their temporal condition has, I fear, a strong tendency to unsettle the poor in their religious and moral condition. I hear some fearful accounts of the infidelity and even atheism… This has been a trial of faith with me…*
>
> Eddington Papers

Barth Blake (d. 1779), William Crowe (d.1805), Joseph Davey (d.1798), William Freek (d.1777) and John Brown (d.1780) were some of those impoverished worstead weavers; James Blake (d.1810) was a shawl manufacturer; James Bateman [d.1806] wove cotton. David Gapp (d.1804) and James Gapp (d.1800) dyed the finished cloth. All these Friends, as examples, are buried in the Gildencroft; there are more than 35 male textile trade employees with recorded graves.

Records of occupations of those interred in the Gildencroft are, agrees our Convener of Archives, "necessarily those of the men." The occupations that we know about, those entered on the index cards in the green metal drawer file were gathered from ledgers and minute books. However hard the women worked over the centuries, juggling all the things women juggle, virtually none of them are credited with any occupation outside the home. They are, if at all, recorded as 'wife of' or 'daughter of'. They may have taken in laundry, or lodgers or children, brewed small beer, been one of the outworkers paid in cash by the visiting foremen from shoe or textile industries. Many women certainly did work; they would have had to in order to make ends meet. They would have got up before dawn to scrub and clean. They would have been called to assist with births and the laying out of the dead.

Susannah Hewett (d.1680) was servant to Antony Alexander and Mari Hunt (d.1682) to Thomas Murford. Two entries are termed "singlewomen" or "spinster" presumably because the women could afford to be but we do not know how they filled their days nor do we know the source of this independent income. Only one man, so far, is credited with "singleman". We find that Mehitabel Tallowen was a schoolmistress. Amelia Opie, we know wrote fiction. Anna Forster and many of the Gurney women were able to

Travel in the Ministry, visiting, bestowing largess because their husbands could afford to pay others to do the housekeeping of their vast houses in their stead. Few of these servants are credited with an occupation beside the entry for their grave, if they have one in the Gildencroft, except Michael Glenton aged 73 in 1807 who seems to have been permitted to retire.

Not many entries of those we can assume were working class have the luxury of "retired" beside their entry. They would have had to work until they dropped. Remember, John Stone and Isaac Harrison dug graves as second occupations almost until they were ready for one themselves. There were no pensions until relatively recently and many of their offspring were as poor as they were.

The jobs done by those who now lie at rest in the Gildencroft? "It's a matter of interpretation by the record gatherer. And some of them worked by Chinese Whispers."

K

Kinship

The Gildencroft Burial Ground is a place where Norwich Meeting gathers to commemorate past Friends, and have done so for over 300 years... you can sit alongside Eric Tebby ...on the bench inscribed with his name. or stay awhile to enjoy the view down the avenue from the newly positioned bench erected in 2012 and built by Michael Harvey.

A fiddler and an accordion player lead a procession on a Winter walk around to visit past Friends, share their memories and enjoy the laughter and music echoing around under the trees.

All these are the ways Norwich Meeting brings the burial ground back into the life of the meeting.

Nigel Wimhurst playing his accordian

The benches in the Gildencroft - the plaque was engraved by David Holgate

Elizabeth Langwade

Friends are asked

in making their Wills to have strict regard to justice and equity and not to be actuated by caprice and prejudice to the injury of those who may have a reasonable expectation from their kindred and near connections. Let none (although occasion may have been given or taken) carry any resentment to the grave, remembering that we all stand in need of mercy and forgiveness. Friends are advised not to make large bequests to relatives or others who do not need them; and to remember the pressing claims of religious and social concerns.

Few Last Will and Testaments remain in the corporate possession of the Religious Society of Friends, but it can be reasonably expected that such documents may form part of such an archive if Quakers received a bequest from them. It is certainly the case with that of Elizabeth Langwade's 1748 will, bequests from which became part of a long standing trust fund and was of great benefit to the Society and individuals around it.

Norfolk Record Office. SF325/1 -

In the name of God Amen. I Elizabeth Langwade of the city of XX [sic] forewith singlewoman being of sound disposing mind and memory so heretofore make and declare this my last will and testament in mannor following (that is to say) I commend my soul into the hands of Almighty God My Creator, and my body I commit to the Earth to be herein decently buried according to the discretion of my executors hereinafter named Joseph Henry Gurney the elder of the city of Norwich, Worstead Weaver, and Henry Kett of the same City, Woolcomber, my executors.

Also I give and bequeath unto my said executors all the mortgages, bill, bonds and notes and securities for monies that shall be in my dwellinghouse only at the time of my decease upon this trust and confidence that thou my executors or the survivor of them shall first pay out thereof the sum of twenty pounds for my funeral expenses incident to the execution of this my will and ten pounds for the care and trouble therein and the residue of said mortgages, bills, bonds and notes and other securities to be paid to the Society of People called Quakers in the said city to be employed and disposed off for sure uses and intents and purposes as the Members of the Monthly Meeting for the time being, and for ever in the said Society shall think moot and approve of.

Also I do hereby order and direct that such person or persons to whom I shall in my lifetime give or deliver any mortgage, bill, bond or note to me made for securing the payment of any sum or sums of money to me at any past or future time, That such person or persons to whom I shall give or deliver the same shall have and enjoy the whole benefit for ever.

And I do hereby order that my executors or the survivor of them shall upon request in due form of Law at the costs and charges of the person or persons requiring the same Assign over such mortgages, bills, bonds or notes to such person or persons as I shall give or deliver the same as he or she or they shall appoint or if occasion shall require that my said executors or the survivor of them shall permit and suffer their or either of their names to be made use of for the recovery and obtaining of the monies due and to grow due on such mortgage, bill, bond or note so to be given or delivered by me as aforesaid. They, my executors and the survivor of them being indemnified for so doing.

Also I give to my Uncle William Langwade one shilling and I give to my Aunt Judith Langwade one shilling.

Also I give and bequeath to my respected Friends Anne Kendale and Sarah Kendale both of the said City, Singlewomen, all my plate, china, household goods and wearing cloths (except my said household and wearing linen) to be equally divided between them. And I give my said household and wearing linen that I shall leave at my decease to my Cousin Susannah, the wife of John Lovelace, apothecary, to her own use for ever.

And lastly I do hereby revoke and make void all former wills and testaments by me at any time heretofore made, published or declared. In witness thereof unto this my last Will and Testament herein contained I the said Elizabeth Langwade, have hereunto set my hand and seal the seventh day of February in the year of Our Lord, one thou-

sand, seven hundred and forty eight.

Elizabeth Langwade.

Signed sealed published and declared by the above named Elizabeth Langwade for her last Will and Testament in the presence of us who have subscribed our names hereunto in her presence and at her request.

Anna Wright. Rich. Inriss.

By the tenor of those present, we Warton Peck, Doctor of Laws, Commissary in and throughout the Archdeaconry of Norwich lawfully constituted, make known to all men that on the fifteenth day of March in the year of Our Lord one thousand, seven hundred and forty eight, before Reverend Thomas Money, Clerk our Surrogate in the City of Norwich in the Archdeaconry aforesaid.

The last Will and Testament of Elizabeth Langwade of the said City of Norwich in our jurisdiction, Singlewoman and deceased, hereunto annexed, was proved, approved and registered and Administration of all and singular, the goods, chattels and Credits of the deceased and anyway concerning her said Will was duly granted to Joseph Gurney the elder and Henry Kett.

Quakers, Executors named in the said Will having first affirmed according to Law well and faithfully to administer the same and to make a true and perfect inventory of all and singular the said goods, chattels and credits and to exhibit the same in the registry of the Archdeaconry of Norwich aforesaid on or before the last day of June next ensuing and also to render a just and true amount when thereto lawfully called.

Given under the seal of offices the day and year first above writ on.

Fran. Spendlove. Deputy Registrar.

Early Quakers, convinced of the relevance of Matthew 5:33-37 and of James 5:12 to everyday life refused to take oaths in courts of law (for which many went to prison), or in many other places, thus precluded them from many professional and public positions. They also saw the need to keep to "Yea" and "Nay" to promote strict standards of integrity in personal and business life thus achieving a reputation for dependability. The Affirmation Acts 1696 and 1722 enabled Quakers to make, in lieu of an oath in most cases when it was required, a solemn Affirmation that they were telling the truth. This right to affirm was gradually extended into a general right, notably by the oaths Act 1888.[1]

The requested inventory of Elizabeth's "said goods, chattels and credits" is not attached to her Will nor to the Probate Document. Financial records show that it cost the Meeting £1-10/- to have the Will probated.

The Will was made very close to the time of Elizabeth's death and we can only surmise what was in her mind at the time. We know very little about her; the family name appears a few times in the Society's Minute Book[2] of the years prior to her death so they were active Quakers.

> *This meeting is acquainted that the sum left is pretty considerable and that there are sundry near relations, children of Robert Blake of Pulham deceased in necessitous circumstances do desire the sum of Ten Pounds and also to William Langwade if living and Judith Langwade or by what other name she may go as that so soon they can conveniently can do bring the account made up...*
>
> Norwich Monthly Meeting 3rd Month 1749

The final amount seems to have been £603/10/11. In making these payments to "sundry near relations" at the outset it may be that the Society avoided arguments. The Trustees had been given the freedom to use this money as they saw fit and, after all, the Aunt and Uncle who had brought her up hadn't been disinherited, cut off without the proverbial shilling. Legally, Elizabeth had ensured that but one has to wonder whether she did, indeed, "carry resentment to the grave." Conversely, was she confident that they were relatives who did not need a large bequest? There is evidence too for this. She most emphatically remembered "the pressing claim of religious and social concern" having left the bulk of her estate for Friends' work.

The bequest to three friends – the first two, Ann and Sarah, certainly Quakers too from the use of the capital F in the Will document- demonstrates for me the emotional bonds amongst the four women, three of them unmarried. All would have use for and care for Elizabeth's personal and household items, keepsakes undoubtedly, but purposeful and practical.

It is possible to follow how Trustees used this bequest from their specially commissioned account ledger[3] the cost of which was recorded as two shillings. Page two records the total deposit of £603-10-11d on February 4th 1750 once all "the mortgages, bills bonds and notes and other

1 Alistair Heron, Quakerspeak

2 N.R.O. SF55

3 N.R.O. SF358/1

securities" had been discharged. One of these bonds was a sum of money that had been lent by Elizabeth in her lifetime to Ann. Its purpose is not recorded. It can be seen that although Elizabeth knew that a bequest of personal and household goods would be welcomed by her respected friend Ann it was not deemed fitting to discharge it either by Elizabeth in the Will or by her executors administering it, nor did Ann ask that it be done. Within twelve months twenty one personal cash payments from ten shillings and six pence to three guineas had been recorded for items ranging from payment of a Church rate of 3/- for Sam Defrance, £1/4/- to James Bray for wine and 10/- for the Beadle Men, together with further disbursements of £4/7/11d by John Gurney to a total of £37/19/11d. What conclusion should one make as to the purpose of these payments, never mind the ten persons named who each received £10. Some of the names suggest that they were unlikely to have been in financial hardship. Nevertheless, one cannot fault the openness of the declared accounting. The remainder of the trust was held in securities by Gurneys Bank.

Gurneys' skilful stewardship of the investment resulted in the Trust Fund growing over the following twelve months to £711/5/0d with the consolidated accounts signed by Samuel Gurney. Over time Gurneys bank ensured that the interest continued to outweigh the payments made and the capital held in securities not needing withdrawal. In may 1779 the interest alone was a colossal £140/19/10d: "being the principal of interest money arising from Elizabeth Langwade's Gift to Norwich Monthly Meeting, one hundred pounds thereof was to remain for the present at an interest of 4% per annum…." The financial report was signed by Nathanial Springall.

The Monthly Meeting of April 1782 records that Norwich Quakers embarked upon investments in land and property using the Gift moneys:

> *Part thereof in the estate in Clements parish in this City now called the Orchard purchased of the late James Dawber and let by this Meeting to Robert Sewell at the rent of twenty pounds per annum, and the other part thereof in the purchase of £200 stock 3% consolidated annuities standing in the joint names of Thomas Standing, Richard Gurney and Thomas Kett*

This report was signed by Isaac Jermyn, Clerk to the Meeting. Exacting record keeping continued as interest and rent received covered amounts paid out to poor Friends as detailed by Overseers.

From an entry of 31st July 1810, 62 years after Elizabeth's death it is possible to begin considering her motives in giving only a shilling each to her Aunt and Uncle. It seems she may indeed have 'taken resentment to the grave'. A payment is recorded of seven guineas to E. Langwade's relations. Was her Will finally questioned by the family? Did Friends concede that there was a worthy case? Payment was recorded always via the same Overseer, B. Candler, sometimes by name 'the Widows Horton and Green' or simply 'E.L.'s Relations' and always the same amount, five guineas, from 1810 to 1831.

In 1826 Norwich Meeting, having contracted to replace their Meeting House in Goat Lane, embarked upon a most grandiose scheme and became greatly overstretched financially by their architect, John Patience. Whilst the final bill came to £7,731/0/0d, their original budget had been just over half that amount. Friends were forced to seek further subscriptions to liquidate money assets and seek help in wider circles throughout the Society.

Investment stock held in the Langwade Gift helped to reduce the debt. The Will did not specify that Elizabeth's bequest be used for charitable purposes only but "...for sure intents and purposes as the members of the Monthly Meeting for the time being and for ever in the said Society shall think moot and approve of...." Personal difficulties in financial affairs were of great shame within the Society of Friends at that time, with a need to preserve the integrity of its outward appearance paramount: Bankruptcy led to forfeiture of membership. Corporate financial embarrassment would have been impossible to concede. Friends would have needed little persuasion to think the use of Langwade's Gift 'moot' and thus approve it.

The balance one hundred years after the Trust's inception was £34/14/8d. Further amounts record in 1837 settlement of bills for Meeting House repairs "...to Robert Pank for laying gas down in Goat Lane Meeting House..." at a cost of £22/5/5d. The Gift's balance had at this time risen again to £118/12/8d.

The final entry in the ledger dated December 31st 1865 records a balance of £12/16/5d which then became consolidated into Friends other Trust Funds. Elizabeth Langwade's money, disregarding any hidden agenda towards her family in the terms of her Will, had been of great benefit to a great many people.

The Manthorpe Family

There are six members of the Manthorpe Family buried in the Gildencroft; Hamilton and his wife Eliza, their daughter Matilda Jermy, their son Walter and his wife and their son, also Walter, whom we knew at Norwich Meeting during the 1990s and 2000s. Much of the late nineteenth century regeneration of the Religious Society of Friends at Goat Lane came through the Adult Schools with the Manthorpe family being a prime example. Hamilton first worked for Alexander Eddington in their grocery shop across from the marketplace.

111, Cambridge Street, Norwich.

Dear sir,

Through the mercy of God, we have been blessed by coming to the school and attending the meetings of friends, on connecting with goat lane. And have felt it our duty to apply that our names may be entered as members of the Society of Friends. If by doing so we can help the cause of Christ and the coming of his Kingdom.

Yours sincerely, Hamilton and Eliza Manthorpe.

N.R.O. SF287/138

The committee appointed to visit Hamilton and Eliza Manthorpe on their application for membership have brought in the following report viz: We have had a satisfactory interview with Hamilton and Eliza Manthorpe. They have not hitherto been in membership with any Christian denomination. Eliza Manthorpe experienced conversion at an earlier period than her husband whose definite religious convictions date from his attendance at the School about 8 years ago. Though he has attended the evening meetings his attendance in the mornings began about 3 yrs since and his wife followed a little later. They are both in full sympathy with us in the Christian views which distinguish us from other denominations, some of which they seem to have adopted before their acquaintance with Friends. We have confidence in recommending the Monthly Meeting to accede to their application. Signed John J. Howes. E.L. Sayer. Henry Brown.

The foregoing report is satisfactory to this meeting and Hamilton and Eliza Manthorpe are hereby recorded as members of our religious Society. John J. Howes is requested to inform them thereof......

Norwich Monthly Meeting 5th Month 1895[1]

Hamilton was drawn firstly to become Class Secretary to Number 3 Class and later to teach a class of his own at the Gildencroft Meeting House. By 1894 he had a class of at least ten lads aged 13 and over who met on Sundays between 2 and 4.30pm and sorely tried his strength.

From this outreach came new employment for Hamilton as Coffee Cart Manager. Cattle drovers brought their animals into Norwich Cattle Market around the castle mound, their main route from the west being along Dereham Road with a stopping point at the Gibraltar Gardens Public House. A grassy loke there allowed the cattle to the river for a drink while the men collected inside the Gibraltar. The journey continued along Charing Cross to St Andrew's Plain to the market. Here stood Manthorpe with one of the seven horse drawn Coffee Carts supplied by Eddingtons intended as a temperate alternative to the many inns surrounding the market. He fulfilled this job for thirty years promoting this ideology until his retirement.

His grandson Walter remembers being allowed to go to the stables with Hamilton very early on Monday mornings to collect the horse and lead it to be hitched to the freshly supplied cart and slowly walk it to the pitch outside St Andrew's Hall. "It was a real treat for a small boy..." he told me once. Then he was allowed to help hose it down and replenish it on Saturday evenings ready for the following week.

During the 1914-1918 war Walter (senior) was imprisoned in Dartmoor as a Conscientious Objector. Afterwards he following his parents' example of health ideals and diet opened one of the first health food shops in Britain in White Lion Street, Norwich. He lived as he advocated and is remembered, in his late eighties, cycling to the office he still retained in the shop. The shop is still there but the business only closed a few years ago.

During the 1939-45 war, Walter (junior)'s brother John, was a spitfire pilot who was shot down and killed. He has his grave in Lakenham Churchyard.

1 N.R.O. SF64

"How did this sit with your parents' beliefs?" I asked our Walter one day after Meeting for Worship. He was a little shakey on his own feet by then so I was carrying his cup of tea, on a saucer with a teaspoon and a biscuit laid to one side. I always felt you never gave Walter a mug; he simply wasn't that sort of man. It went with laundered and starched shirts and impeccable silk ties.

"They never imposed their beliefs," he replied. "We were left to make up our own minds. I used to be friends with Nugent Monk of the Maddermarket Theatre you know and we used to go out after performances. Father never drank himself but would wait up for me to come home. Nothing was ever said. He didn't chide me for the sherry Monk and I had probably shared. He knew I knew his views but he wasn't going to impose them on me. He was going to allow me to make my own decisions. Once he knew I was home safely, Father would wish me goodnight and go up to bed…"

Our Walter was proud to have been a pupil at the City of Norwich Grammar School in the 1930s, later becoming a member of its Old Boys Association. He enjoyed his time at the school and benefitted greatly. I remember his chuckle as he told me about the reunion he had just been to and his bemusement at being singled out as the oldest Old Boy. There was actually great satisfaction overlaying that bemusement.

Walter qualified as a surveyor with a Norwich firm by the age of twenty, then. Making use of his considerable talent, he moved to London to take up a post in the Office of Works. One local clergyman describing Walter as a young man said "he was robust, principled and practical and sought a series of activities where he could be intellectually stimulated." He lived in a residential club called Youth House established by a group of Theosophists and Internationalists. These people advocated economic and political co operation amongst nations for the benefit of everyone and are beliefs that Walter cherished for the rest of his life. There he met Ann who was to become his wife.

In the years leading up to the Second World War, Jewish refugees were streaming over to England from Europe to escape persecution by the Nazis. Youth House gave great support to those immigrants who mostly hoped they could continue their education in British universities. When the students found that this was not to be so and they faced interment, Walter and Ann found new ways to keep them safe and occupied.

By now "in a government job requisitioning properties" which was relocated to Lancashire when war broke out, Walter told me, that he felt moved one evening to attend a Peace Movement meeting but was observed by a superior on coming out. He was summarily sacked the following morning.

"The Anti War Brigade wasn't condusive to a government job. You couldn't do both", Walter said.

Walter's affirmation as a Conscientious Objector was one of the first to be recognised on philosophical grounds. He was sent to work with the Welsh Forestry Commission, the Fen Drainage Authority around Kings Lynn and to build cottages on the Sandringham Estate. It was at this point that his brother John was killed. After the funeral at Lakenham, Walter felt his views on Conscientious Objection were sorely questioned. Mrs Manthorpe told me that he was in such a turmoil about it all that he was unable to talk at all for six months.

At the end of that war, Walter joined the Central Office of Information, took further building studies and got his Town Planning Qualifications. In 1951 he was involved with the whole Festival of Britain site on the south

WALTER FREDERICK
MANTHORPE
BORN 15TH OF THE 11TH MONTH
1916
DIED 13TH OF THE 6TH MONTH
2007

bank of the Thames, its format and structure. Later, on behalf of the then London County Council he won the contract to design the now familiar Dry Dock for the Cutty Sark at Greenwich. At Crystal Palace, Walter's scheme to reopen the old racing tracks was warmly received giving him the enviable opportunity to become associated with Stirling Moss and Formula One racing.[2]

Walter, it seems, was never one to let any opportunity pass him by and the world was now at his feet. Through the auspices of the Planning Commission, he was "headhunted". This was Walter's apologetic expression in conversation with me. "I'm afraid that's how it was... They did come looking for me." He took his family to Toronto in Canada where began his involvement with the long term plan for the city. He advised upon the choice of design for the new City Hall and as was remarked at his funeral "it is a hallmark of his ability that it is still there." Through Walter's guidance the city is one of the most cosmopolitan and attractive cities in North America. He was particularly fond and proud of the waterfront development on which he worked with Walter Gropius, one of the founding fathers of Modernism.

His son and daughter returned to England for their secondary education at boarding school. His son still remembers the excitement of the journey by Atlantic liner for often they were allowed to travel in the care of the crew. "Father trusted us," I've heard him say. He has remained in Canada and is a renowned journalist and war correspondent. Walter and Ann's daughter, came back to England with her parents and has continued her father's work in town planning and conservation.

Within his professional life, Walter was always extremely sensitive to the needs of the community. In Toronto's Chinatown where whole sweeps of the city were to be cleared, he endeared himself to the residents by listening to them and succeeding in keeping the local culture and flavour such as they wanted. Again in South Ontario, Walter was involved with the Hudson Bay scheme at Garlick Hill. Similarly back in Britain, the city of Glasgow was planning to replace large tracts of housing. Walter was brought in as Consultant for Central Glasgow. "All it needed was a bath and a little loving care....". Much of The Gorbals tenements survive.

Walter was inspired by his convictions, much of them inherited from his father and grandfather, leaving a large imprint: "A substantial gift to humanity....". The reading at his funeral service in St Stephen's Church was most apt.

---

2 Having been driven through Norwich's narrow medieval street pattern by Walter in his last year of driving his great heavy Mercedes I can testify that he never lost that reckless love of speed.

The gifts and the challenges that Jesus has to offer allow us to be fulfilled in life and make the most of our time on earth....We must develop the stewardship of our time and talents...

Walter did all of that all of the time and delighted in others doing the same regardless of the fact that towards the end of his life he began to lose both his hearing and his sight. He never came into formal membership of the Society of Friends; his father was already born when Hamilton and Eliza's membership was given so there was no Birthright. Nevertheless, both the Walters were in complete sympathy with Quaker testimonies and led their lives accordingly.

The Walter we all knew was a most self effacing man and volunteered little of his life's work to his Ffriends here genuinely believing it to be of little importance and of no interest to others. As we came to know him some of the façade slipped away and the full life he had led started to become apparent. He found Quakers a peculiar people –and so we are- and initially had difficulties with our equalities between genders. He was uncomprehending and disbelieving that there was always a friend out there who would genuinely delight in his company. Eventually he became an enthusiastic Doorkeeper and Welcomer. "What else can a doddery old man do?" he would say. When one enquired how he was today his reply was invariably "Oh, coping, you know."

Walter Frederick Manthorpe was laid to rest in the Gildencroft Burial Ground on June 21st 2007 beside his parents, his Aunt Matilda Jermy and her husband and his grandparents.

N

Mable's Marigolds

Mable Violet Nicholl 1911-2011

Condensed in part from TESTIMONY TO THE GRACE OF GOD AS SEEN IN THE LIFE OF MABLE NICOLL, the original text of which was compiled by Frances Warns and Danene Rogers and is kept with the Meeting's minutes.

Mable was born in Ipswich in 1911, trained as a pupil teacher and taught P.E. and country dancing in Wickham Market. She then moved to Plymouth and later still, Loughborough. After World War 2 she was a youth leader at Bottisham College in Cambridgeshire and led many Youth Hostelling holidays. She particularly liked walking and cycling in the Lake District.

Her name first appears in Quaker membership lists in 1948 in Luton and a year later she moved to Asford, then to Norfolk in 1963 to be matron at Wymondham College, the Local Authority Boarding School. We learn that at work she was a strict disciplinarian, stood for no nonsense; we all of us who knew her experienced this. But she got things done, made people see practical wise sense and we loved her for it and in spite of it.

She spent her days off with her nieces and nephews and in the school holidays when they would camp in an old army bell tent. When the family had saved up enough to buy a caravan they went to Beeston near Sheringham. Nobody else, the children remembered, could camp beside the sea from Easter to October Half Term.

Her niece Sally remembers with delight that at the College, as well as everything else, Aunty was in charge of the school tuckshop. During the school holidays they used to accompany her to the wholesalers and feast their eyes. She remembers Aunty saving part of her own food ration to help the family and often being there waiting for them to get home from their own school.

She was a good organiser and soon in charge of Quaker Sales at Goat Lane, with her fine white hair often in danger of becoming unpinned, apron on and her little dog skitting about her heels. That is how many friends who were very young then remember her. Though she never had any of her own, Mable obviously loved children. She took care of the Children's Meeting in Norwich and as a Prison Visitor looked after the children of those who came to the Club for families of inmates of Norwich Prison and while wives visited their husbands.

In the mid 1970s Mable had her picture in the papers with her great friend Mary Pottenger when the City Council was attempting to clear Travellers families off land in Costessey. There they stood, these two Grande Dames, straight backed and Mable with her beloved dog, Kirsty, in her arms, supportive to the last.

All her life Mable was true to her testimonies of simplicity and truth and showed her love of the earth, nature, trees and flowers. When she retired she moved into her bungalow in Costessey, her first permanent home where she created a beautiful garden and was a founder member of the Flower Club there. Mable lived a good Quaker life in that there was nothing extravagant. That bungalow was simply furnished and welcoming with geraniums flowering on the windowsill all year round… [The last of them, ones that she had kept growing for years and others grown from cuttings still flourish in the porch at the Meeting House.] …Most of the surfaces in her little home were scattered with small objects that were special to her.

Mable was a keen flower arranger and used to produce vasefulls for funerals, weddings, festivals and parties at Goat Lane. She was a keen member of the Patchwork and Quilting Group for many years and when she was no longer able to join in, her sight and her fingers letting her down, the quilters made her a flower quilt that was on her bed until the day she died.

She accepted people from all walks of life and treated them with equality. She spoke truthfully about how she felt; this could be hurtful but showed her strength of character.

Mable hadn't intended that she would end her days in the Gildencroft Burial Ground. She had always said she wanted her body to be used for medical research.

"Useful to the end," we said.

"And practical."

"And economical!" as the researchers dispose of the remains.

When her time came, in her hundredth year, there wasn't a research programme in the area that would take her body; she hadn't died in hospital. Eventually the Alzheimers programme at Addenbrookes Hospital in Cambridge was pleased to receive her brain to have perhaps an indication of how it was possible to live a long and useful life without a hint of dementia. So very early one morning two Quakers and one nephew, Tim, attended the cremation she had never planned to need. Her simple wooden coffin was warmly wrapped in a scarlet wool blanket decorated with the faces of South American children. We spoke lovingly to Mable, to eachother of our memories of her and left her a few tall blue poppies from Tim's garden still with the morning's dew on them.

On the day we scattered her ashes across the Gildencroft, amongst old

Friends, around their headstones, about all their final resting places, we realised we had created a winding lifeline of vivid orange. She and Sally had compiled a long list of names in preparation for this day. We scraped off moss and lichens from the carved lettering on some of the stones, pulled up handfuls of groundsel and took great care not to disturb the wildflowers. You only had to have seen Mable's beloved bungalow garden to know that she believed, by and large, that flowers should be left to grow where The Good Lord put them! Sally had mixed marigold petals with the ashes "...signifying the good healing in Aunt Mable's life...There's a lot of healing powers in marigold flowers...."

Mable, in her hundredth year, had outlived her contemporaries and had waited, she said, a long time to be reunited. Mable Nicholl went a long way to heal a lot of us.

Amelia Opie

Amelia Alderson, born in Norwich in November 1769, was the much-loved only child of Doctor James Alderson of Colgate. He was one of a group intelligentsia connected with the Octagon Unitarian Chapel during the late eighteenth and early nineteenth century. Seen by friends and family as a "charming child [with] a great love for learning". Amelia's "education was devoted mainly to French, music and dancing." She swung between seriousness and frivolity in equal parts, loving to "compose and perform songs for visitors..." winning a great number of admirers. When still quite young she was so sorry for the inmates of Bedlam, the Bethel Hospital, that she bought them flowers and threw them over the wall.

The Aldersons were friends with the Gurney family then living at Magdalen Court and the solitary Amelia loved the company of all the Gurney children. She was a frequent visitor to their subsequent home out at Earlham Hall.

James Alderson stood for Parliament in 1773 and lost by a single vote:

> *thrown out by the same means that many an election has been lost, viz. his Friends being oversecure*
>
> Thomas Bland to John Gurney [1]

Mrs Alderson died when the child was fifteen so Amelia immediately assumed the position of head of her father's household and took on a prominent place in his intellectual circle. Alderson told his daughter

> *Amelia, your mother is gone; may you never have reason to blush when you remember her*

---

1 Eddington manuscript

It is said that "she was the pride and darling of his home and throughout her long life her father's approbation was the chief motive of her existence…."

Amelia enjoyed writing, both poetry and novels, and her work suggests that since her mother died while Amelia was still young the most vivid parental memories she had retained might have been of punishment.

And when a mother's firm, yet mild, reproof
Had sent me, pale and tearful, to my room,
and his smile
Seemed to reward when that fond mother came
To hear her child's contrition, and forgive

Later examples of her writings were dramatized and following a visit of the famous Mrs Siddons to the City, Amelia developed and maintained an interest in the theatre all her life. London was a great attraction for her and she paid frequent visits to the capital where she was much admired for her beauty, brilliant conversation and literary gifts.

Letters home reveal that she included people such as William Godwin and Mary Wollstonecraft in her circle.

I wish to remind them that a weak hand is as able as a powerful one to hold a mirror in which we may see any defects in our dress or person.

This prim passage demonstrates Amelia's attempts to help others recognise their moral failings and rectify the human character. Instead of subscribing to Godwin's radical opinions on marriage, or other such notions amongst his associates, Amelia held fast to her own beliefs.

She met many men who professed romantic interests towards her; Thomas Holcraft, an artist for whom she sat for a portrait; Lord Brougham, James Mackintosh. In 1797 she met John Opie, a painter and the youngest child of a Cornish carpenter. He had been unhappily married and was recently divorced. Amelia saw that he had an excellent brain and a gift for painting which his friend, the noted satirist Dr Walcott, likened to that of Rembrant. Opie produced portraits of many famous people of his day, became court painter and had work hung in the Royal Academy. John fell in love with Amelia immediately, dressed as she was in blue and wearing a hat with three feathers in it over her auburn curls. She said of him:

Often do I rationally and soberly state to Opie the reasons that might urge me to marry him – in time – and the reasons why I could never be happy with him, nor he with me. But it always ends in his persisting in his suit....

After much persistence on Opie's part and hesitation on Amelia's part they were married in London on May 8th 1798 at Marylebone Church. John was not fond of society and urged Amelia to write in order to keep her at home:

He knew that my most favourite amusement was writing and he always encouraged my ambition to become an acknowledged author. Our only quarrel on the subject was not that I wrote so much but that I did not write more and better. And to the last hour of my existence I shall deplore those habits of indolence which made me neglect to write while it was in my power to profit by his criticisms and advice, and when, by employing myself more regularly in that manner, I should have been sure to receive the proudest and dearest reward of woman... a husband's admiration.

In 1801 her novel 'The Father and Daughter' was published with immediate success. It was translated into French and Portugese and formed the basis for a play in which Fanny Kemble appeared. Her novel, Adeline Mowbray (1802), believed to be inspired by Mary Wollstonecraft's life, followed and Amelia's fame was securely established. She was sought out by the wealthy, the titled and the learned alike and her charming personality made her a general favourite.

John tragically died from "swelling of the brain" at the early age of 45 in 1807 and was buried in St Paul's Cathedral. Amelia returned to Norwich where she kept her father's house and renewed her friendships with the Gurneys. She began to spend eight to ten hours a day on her writing, hoping to divert herself from the loss of her husband. She became especially attracted to Joseph John by whom she was greatly influenced during the rest of her life. Gurney frequently tried to turn her from her frivolous way of life. Her love of pleasure was too strong, however, and she soon resumed her visits to London becoming absorbed into the gay social life once again. Some impression by the devout Gurneys must have been made though and she was further influenced by the most renowned of the Earlham daughters, Elizabeth Fry, who by this time had begun her work at Newgate Prison.

In 1821, John Alderson became seriously ill so Amelia returned once more to Norwich and nursed her father devotedly for four years. Joseph

John Gurney was a frequent visitor to the doctor and through his ministry Alderson renounced his lifelong scepticism and accepted the Christian faith. He died in October 1825 and was buried in the very top left hand corner of Gildencroft in the shelter of the wall. Amelia described how even eleven years later the grave was "blue with forgetmenots… flourishing there which S. Martin will attend to."

Citing the care and comfort which Joseph John had given to her father at the time of his last illness, Amelia became seriously interested in Quaker beliefs and was received into membership of the Religious Society soon after. Her whole manner of life changed. She abandoned her novels and wrote instead a series of moral stories. The moral stories were not a riotous success. However, it seems that she was not averse to having her novels republished both in this country and America and accepting the income from those editions.

Amelia went travelling (because she could afford it!) Unlike Anna Forster whose Travelling in The Ministry took her where she could promote the Quaker ethos, Amelia's travels, were for pleasure and entertainment and no small degree of 'name dropping'. From Paris, 16th June 1829, she wrote to Joseph John Gurney:

Rue Cadet no 11 faux, M-Martre.

At length my dear friend I have found leisure to write to thee but I fear my letter will not be worth the price of the postage. I will not dwell on the roughness of our passage, which, as it did not make me ill, I enjoyed.

I will content myself with saying that I had a companion Wilhelmina Taylor, a young beautiful Irish Friend whom I consented to take under my care to Paris, malgre me. She was going to a pension, a catholic one, & was waiting in London for someone to take her as she was fixed to go, in order, by her mother's desire, to qualify herself to return to teach in her Mother's School, it was well she should go under good care and I saw her safe into the hands of Madselle [sic] Alex… But enough of this.

The first thing I did ye day after my arrival was to send my letters as addressed which Dr. Hodgkin had kindly given me. I also wrote to the Dutchess de Broglie to announce my arrival. Sarah and I then drove to the Jardin des Plantes; as we passed the Place de Greve we saw the gens d'armes out and turning our heads to ye right, we beheld the Guillotine. A man was going to be executed for murder, murder of his wife, - but not of an hour. As our coachman wanted to do something to his wheel, we alighted and made our way thro' ye crowd to one of the gens d'armes, who said Entrez mesdames, en faite la tom. We did so, & approached, and looked at this terrible machine, with a sickness at heart, a feeling I can't describe. I asked if it had at all changed its form since the time of the revolution, but he said No, not at all, & then, having seen all we could, we returned to our fiacre… At the Jardin we saw the elephant bathe and a very interesting sight it was. The giraffe we admired very much, but my pet was l'aigle destructeur, the grandest bird I ever saw, he was of black and white, and had a sort of tuft on its head, like a cockatoo. We had not time to see the museum.

The next day (1st day) I took a fiacre and called Wilhelmina Taylor by her desire to convey her to ye Champs Elisees, to Isaac Sargeant's house where the Friends assemble. I found her dressed a Capausienne which did not become her. She was not used to it, & her hat, & ornaments of bright and singled colours and her white gloves seemed to impede her motions and engross her wholly. I was pleased with I.S.'s wife, our meeting consisted of the three amiable Stephensons (not dressed like Friends) William Payne, the father of Dr Payne, a man of coarse manner, knowing his history I did not feel him an acquisition to us, Nathaniel Cosin of Southampton and Arnold Buffon the American and ye Sergeants and their son. A motley group but I trust some of us felt unity, and that our hour of silent sitting, for it was no more, was favoured. But how short! The wife afterwards told me that when there was only her husband & two more they read a psalm & a chapter and then sat in silence, but as there were so many of us they had not done so that day. I told her I could not think it necessary any day, & that if I sat with only one friend, I could have no unity with the custom at all.

Dr Railbot came to fetch us & we walked thro' ye Champs Elisees, ye Tuilleries & the Place de Vendome in our way to a fiacre. What a walk! My young friend had seen nothing of Paris before (I dare not show it to her) & was much pleased, as much as her troublesome big hat would let her be…

That day when I returned, I found Jornand of ye Institut had called on me and his wife, leaving a note inviting me to accompany the latter to the Institut Royale to the coming Séance of the Academy where deux eloges were to be pronounced, one by Baron Cuvier on Bose ye Naturalist, & one by Laurien ye great Chemist on La Place. I was to go by appointment that morning (2nd day) to ye Dutchess de Broglie, however I found I could do both, & I did both. I much enjoyed my visit to Albertine de Broglie. She asked me many questions concerning Friends and I have promised to send her thy book; she said she had read Clarkson and to ye translation of Clarkson she had written a preface, she

writes charmingly. When I left her she was going to some prison to see a poor man. She asked me very often if I was happy, I assured her that I was so, that I had found la paix; she said it did not always follow that a religious cause made one paisable. !

... We found the hall crowded, but got good places. I had to undergo many presentations and flatteries, for as an author I am as much known and more admired perhaps than in England; one thing annoyed me particularly, I was introduced to men, celebrated authors, of whom I had never heard! Not of late years being much read in modern French authors. I was comforted to find one person there as remarkable as myself in appearance. An Egyptian in his picturesque dress.........The eloges were eloquent & I understood most of them but badly delivered.

... This morning by appointment I had a visit from Nath. Cosin and Arnold Buffon and then came Mary Stephenson and we four went to call on La Fayette, with my letter of introduction to him. He was out and ye man & I go tomorrow at ten. M.S. and I then went to ye Louvre which gave me a melancholy pleasure, from associations of former times. I then returned Madame Jornand's visit, who makes much of me... This evening, Mary Stephenson takes me to an American Lady's, a Friend of ye name of Hicks who is very ill, but wishes to see me, not nearly related to Elias Hicks, if at all.

I will not close this until tomorrow.

4th day 17th. I was delighted with my visit to friend Hicks, I found her a pious, resigned, suffering woman, who had been to Nice in search of health, and having thus done all she can to live, is contented, if so her creator, willing to die 7 she is going back to New York, via England. She is attended by a son and a daughter. The former was going to La

Fayette's weekly Soiree. Il recoit a 9 heures all the Americans & others, & appears surrounded by his children & grandchildren... The room in which we were has four very long glasses in it. The others, they say, are equally good. Arnold Buffon read us a letter of his addressed to La Societe de la Morale Chretienne, founded here by Joseph Price, which prospers... Farewell for the present. This letter is to go to England with Sargeant's pleasing wife tomorrow.

1 o clock. Just returned, a most pleasing reception from the marquis, I was almost naughty enough to wish I had gone alone, or only with Sarah perhaps. My friends at first talked all, but he at length had the conversation to himself and spoke in English 7 as well as I could on Slavery in America & so on. He said his daughters should call on me to invite me to his house next 3rd day eve: was most kind, et flatteur. He is a handsome and becoming man of 72 & quite highbred! He is a man to love.

With dear love to all, thy very aff. A. O.

J. J. wrote from Toronto of her fame in America and that her works on lying and detraction were much valued:

Friends particularly express their good opinion of them. They would greatly enjoy seeing thee here…

Nevertheless in 1844 he censured her severely for authorising a reprint of her works. Amelia was unabashed:

It would give me an opportunity of correcting whatever I deemed amiss in the said publications… I never thought, nor do I now think, that in doing this I have at all violated my engagements as a Friend… Many of my religious friends and more than one Friend said they thought I had done right, and a pious lady & she is the editor of serious books has written to me expressing pleasure at this reprint…

Amelia and Joseph John corresponded freely and extensively and spent a lot of time together. Their companionship obviously caused much speculation both inside and outside their families. His daughter Anna wrote in 1841 to Eliza Kirkbride:

Papa was in London all 4th day after calling on A. Opie – and expecting to see some flowers, was enticed by her to a Botanic Garden, which turned out to be a most fashionable promenade where they paraded together to their mutual satisfaction. On their way they met Lady Colebrook who asked Papa if that was the lady (meaning A. Opie) whom he was going to marry…

Amelia and J.J.s relationship did not progress beyond strong friendship. In fact, Gurney's third wife, who outlived him, was Eliza.

The deaths of Elizabeth Fry and Joseph John Gurney shadowed Amelia's later years but in 1847 she moved into the small house off Castle Meadow that still bears a plaque to her memory. She wrote sadly of how she was forced to explain this move to her staff, some of whom would no longer be needed. Her former worldly friends saw little of her while she lived quietly in Norwich, devoting herself to good works, principally Anti Slavery campaigns, prison reform and the Bible Society. In spite of having to adopt the rather severe Quaker dress and practices of the time, Amelia always retained her warmth and enthusiasm for life remaining active to the end. When over eighty years old she rode from the Assizes beside the Judge in his coach. On her last two visits to London she saw the exiled French Empress and visited the Great Exhibition in 1851 even though she had to be pushed round in a wheelchair.

Popular though Amelia Opie's novels were in her day they have not stood the test of time. Their strong moral purpose outweighed their literary value and their sentiment failed to survive the age in which they were written. The author herself was a far more striking and interesting personality than any of the characters she created.

Amelia Opie died on December 2nd 1853 and was buried beside her father in the Gildencroft.

P

Peace, Politics, Privateers and Posh Frocks

As early as 1620 Norwich weavers had adopted the skills to produce the 'new draperies' and were selling 'Norwich Stuff' to Spain, Portugal. Italy and France. This was cloth of a very high quality, later enforced by the Norwich Worsted Weavers Company which itself was established by act of Parliament in 1650. A century later the city had developed a wide range of high quality fabrics which were brightly coloured, glossy and stiff. Norwich became widely known for its shawls which, initially hand embroidered, were woven for export. The Gurney family's wealth was built on Norwich textile industry.

The researcher is hampered by the singular lack of imagination in the naming of the Gurney children. Families were large with as many as eight or ten surviving children; the eldest son in many generations seemingly called John, who subsequently married a Catherine (or Rachel or Hannah at a pinch!). For example, it is recorded that when Eliza Paul became Joseph John Gurney's third wife and moved into Earlham Hall with her two step-children John Henry and Anna and her sister-in-law Catherine she also acquired no less than one hundred and nineteen nephews and nieces.

In order to keep the fortune within the family, it often meant that close cousins married. It was necessary in order to keep their membership of the Society of Friends that their spouse also had to be in membership. Many infants were named after other members of the family perhaps in order to please a potential godparent. Richenda Gurney was named for her Uncle Richard (1743-1811) who was the principal director of both the bank and of the textile company, Gurney and Bland.

Although the local textile trade at its height was mainly good it was unstable. It was men like John Gurney, the Weaver's Advocate, who revealed the distress of the woollen workers in times of war and in the face of foreign competition when the cheap cotton calico flooded the English market. From his house in St Augustines, he travelled to London to plead their cause in parliament. His outstanding success resulted in laws making it punishable by a £5 fine to actually wear calico clothing. Sir Robert Walpole himself was so impressed by Gurney's speech that he offered John a seat in the Commons. This was refused supposedly because of Quaker views, but Gurney became a local hero. The family itself were of the first to benefit, both financially and by reputation, from this new legislation and engravings were produced of him inscribed:

> *The Woollen Manufacturers' Glory. To the immortal praise of John Gurney of Norwich, who by his extempore speeches February 1720, before ye Honourable House of Commons, turned the scale of contention between the woollen and linen manufacturers.*

This substantial Gurney family fortune (supposedly at one time second only to the Bank of England itself) from textiles enabled the brothers, John and Henry, to start their bank in 1775.

> *We hear that a new Banking House is proposed to be shortly established in this city on a new plan, where good bills on any part of Great Britain or Ireland will be exchanged for drafts on London, or discounted for cash on reasonable terms, and bills being negotiated at the most favourable exchange on London; or business of any kind connected with an undertaking will be conducted with secrecy safety and speed......*
>
> Norwich Mercury 11th February 1775

> *...The Norwich and Norfolk bank will be opened on Saturday 13th inst in St Augustine's where the public may depend on having every accommodation consistent with such an undertaking...*
>
> Norwich Mercury 6th May 1775

In the event of a sudden rush to withdraw deposits such a bank would have nothing left to draw upon other than the private fortunes of its partners, however, Gurney's bucked the trend and by 1777 Bartlett Gurney was able to take over Alderman Poole's fine Georgian house at 3 Redwell Plain and change it to banking use. Poole had been a wine merchant and Gurneys converted the wine cellars into safes for bags of bullion and chests of plate. By 1800 the bank was a local landmark and Redwell Plain had been renamed Bank Plain.

The nature of banking, where men were entrusted with not only their customers' money but also with their family and financial secrets fitted the character of those in the Society of Friends . They were reserved and cautious, kind and truthful, high principled and well disciplined. This did not necessarily mean that they were popular, but early struggles and hardships had contributed to the development of qualities of industry, endurance and clear thinking. Branches were opened in Great Yarmouth, which was of great use with the shipping offices in the same port; Kings Lynn, Halesworth and Wisbeach at a time when it was unusual for a country bank to have more than one office. Elizabeth Isichel (in Victorian Quakers 1970) believes Friends' rejection of the pleasures and ambitions of their society allowed them to direct their energies more single-mindedly to the pursuit of wealth.

The yarns spun in Norfolk were no longer enough to keep the Norwich weavers in employment so the family's cloth company diversified in the late 1770s into the importation of linen fibre and raw hemp from Southern Ireland. It was brought round the coast by small sailing ships into the port of London then up to Norfolk via Great Yarmouth and up into Norwich by barge. The journey by road took ten days in summer and much longer in winter; by sea, the voyage was pretty much governed by wind, or lack of it, and tide. In theory it was quicker though crews had to contend with widespread sandbanks and shoals. The extra journey upstream by keel not only added to the cost but laid cargoes open to theft.

Richard Gurney, as a director of both the family bank and the newly acquired textile company, travelled to Southern Ireland to meet their suppliers. He wrote cautiously to his brother, John Junior:

> *I receive this day my Mother's affectionate letters*[1] *- they will be answered by mine...I have been about this business all this day, nothing else.... I hope we shall be able to leave by the end of this week... Appearances today are very warlike – tho' even upon the Reports of Intelligent People very little is to be gathered.*
>
> 27th November 1770. Eddington Papers

The uncertainty about war continued and affected trade enormously. It also taxed the Quaker mind and the ramifications of The Quaker Peace

1 His mother's letter had been a letter from a mother who had forgotten, as mothers do, that her beloved son was now into his middle years. Perhaps he did not need to be reminded to take care crossing a 'precarious' sea in a 'rigurous' season but he may well have appreciated the recipe for preventing sea sickness. "...I shall not enjoy much Peace", she wrote, ".... until I see thee safe on the English shore....."

BARTLETT GURNEY
DIED 24TH OF 2ND MONTH
1803
AGED 47 YEARS

Testimony. Gurney and Bland were importing vast quantities of linen and hemp but had no control over how it was used once it was sold on. For it to be used in the manufacture of sails and rope for fishing boats or coastal craft was permissible but there was no way of them preventing it being used on Naval Ships which in turn would be turned against an enemy, and John Gurney junior agreed that "Appearances today are very warlike."

Notwithstanding the ever present Quaker pacifist ethic of the war, bankers were still bankers. As early as 1770 with the very real possibility of war at any moment Richard wrote "should there be a war… great advantage will be made with Government security." Later, at the prospect of peace which Richard did not live to see, Cousin Bartlett Gurney (1756-1803) recorded having bought "…40,000 scrip, 3% at 65 and a quarter, since when they rose… the definite treaty being signed that I think there is no doubt of stocks rising" For a Bank, apparently the threat of war and the event of peace were equally profitable!

In 1803 it was expected that Napoleon would try to invade England by landing on the Norfolk coast. John Gurney of Earlham, father of Joseph John and Elizabeth (later Fry), kept four carriages constantly waiting ready to take his family to the relative safety of Ely should the invasion come. There were national calls for subscriptions to fund militia volunteers. Hudson Gurney sent such a donation in contravention of the Quaker Testimony to Peace. When this was reported to Norwich Friends, his membership of the Society was terminated. Young John Gurney, of the Earlham Gurneys actually made to join the Volunteers. His membership was also terminated.

A public syndicate had been established for the purpose of fitting out privateering ships at Yarmouth:

> *… and gentlemen who were willing to encourage the scheme were invited to sign the subscription papers, duplicates of which were lying at messrs Gurneys, Bankers &ct. The shares were fixed at £25 each.*
>
> Norfolk Chronicle Nov 14th 1778

As men of peace, Gurneys could not lend their name to a warlike enterprise therefore John lost no time in issuing a statement on behalf of the entire Gurney family:

> *Having observed an advertisement in the Norwich papers promoting a subscription for the fitting out of Privateers… I find that my kinsman, with whom I am connected in business, upon it being unexpectedly proposed to him had inadvertently assented without due con-*

sideration. Our firm was inserted without my knowledge and consent; and as it is inconsistent with our religious principles for us to be in any way actively concerned in aiding or assisting towards the promotion of such measures as are of a violent or destructive nature we request that notice may be taken that we cannot receive subscriptions to such a purpose.

The war with France was greatly affecting trade, the livelihoods of both the Irish woolcombers and hemp growers and the weavers of Norfolk. The standing Member of Parliament for Norwich, William Windham, was also the Minister for war. Bartlett decided to stand against him at the next election and came within an inch of unseating him.

Throughout his life, Joseph John Gurney had made it a rule never to interfere in politics but in 1833, during the election for the County of Norfolk he made a speech against slavery. His cousin, Thomas Fowell Buxton was engaged with William Wilberforce and others in a campaign for its abolition. It is recorded that the speech "attracted considerable attention..."

Samuel Gurney, entered the counting house of his brother-in law Joseph Fry at fourteen and his whole life became devoted to the business of banking. After his marriage in 1808 with his cousin Elizabeth Sheppard, the wealth which he inherited from his father-in law and his own father had ensured him rapid progress as a partner in the firm of Richardson, Overend, Gurney and Co which for forty years was the greatest discounting house in the world. In the financial "panic" of 1825, the company lent money to other houses becoming known as the Bankers' Bank. In 1856, around the time of the death of Samuel who himself was worth £800,000, it was calculated to have assets worth eight million pounds.

Gurney's bank, Gurney and Overend crashed in 1866 with far reaching consequences. The failure of the bank was mentioned in The Friend because of the connection of so many of its members, as shareholders, or depositors and some of them as directors.

In 1693, William Penn had written

Chuse thy cloaths by thine own eye, not anothers. The more simple and plain they are the better. Neither unshapely nor fantastical; and for use and decency and not for pride.....

Some Fruits Of Solitude. 1693

That is to say, do not be a slave to fashion. The dilemma that the enormously rich Gurneys had was to wear an outfit that was suitable for the

J. J. Gurney

The UK £5 note showing Elizabeth Fry

occasion that did not compromise their Quaker testimony to Simplicity. They were the richest bankers in the City of London, they attended at Court, their peers expected them to dress accordingly.

Louisa Gurney (Mrs Samuel Hoare) wrote on June 5th 1797:

In the evening I dressed in Quaker things but I felt far too ashamed to say or act anything... so strong was the influence of the Quaker spirit. The same seven brothers and sisters sat in a row in front of the Ministers' Gallery at Norwich Meeting... One day Betsy [the future Elizabeth Fry] had on a pair of new purple boots laced with scarlet. Which sounds amazingly gorgeous to us at this day.

The Quaker: A Study in Costume. Amelia Mott Gunmer.

Nevertheless Richenda Gurney asserted (in 1803) that:

All except the plainest of Quakers made some concession to the mode...."

Pricilla Gurney writing to her sister Hannah[later Mrs Buxton] remembered that "Richenda and I wore our dark gowns every day and our aprons in the evenings...." In 1807 it was recorded that the Buxtons' house on the day of the wedding was "overrun with bridemaids in muslin cloaks and chip hats..."

Louisa Gurney remembered that she used to see her sister Elizabeth "in a pink gown attending to all her flock in the dining room...." Gunmer believes that the gown was probably a pattern similar to the lesser calicos and printed stuffs popular at the time. Joseph Fry described the outfit she wore first time he saw his future wife as "...a brown silk gown with a black lace veil bound about the head like a turban, the ends pendent on one side of her face and contrasting with her beautiful light brown hair..."

Katherine Fry remembered that:

Our aunts Catherine and Rachel wore no caps but a headdress of crepe folded turbanwise. Both were brown in the mornings; in the afternoons, Aunt C's were dark red; Aunt R's white. Aunt R also frequently wore white muslin dresses. They had few or no ornament. Aunt C always wore dark or black silk but often with a red shawl. Aunt Pricilla, as a Friend, was dressed in a dark silk or poplin gown exquisitely neat finished and refined...

The real test for her mother, Katherine recalls, was when she was summoned to Court to meet Queen Charlotte at the Mansion House. Hare (The Gurneys of Earlham) describes the clothing dilemma of both women: "Royalty offered its need of approval at the shrine of mercy and good work." Queen Charlotte was just as much in awe of Fry because of her work that she did not want to appear too over decorated. Fry, it appears, was unconcerned and wore her usual uncompromising plain dress. The Queen was small and "covered in diamonds..." while Elizabeth's simple dress added to the height of her tall figure. The meeting was described as

They [Fry's party] entered, Lady Harcourt in full court dress, on the arm of Alderman Wood in scarlet gown; and then the Bishop of Gloucester[2] in lawn sleeves leading our darling mother in her plain Friends cap, one of the light scarf cloak worn by Plain Friends, and a dark silk gown...

In a 1812 letter to Elizabeth, Joseph John Gurney, then aged 23, feared

that neither of us will soon get mates exactly to suit us; and for my part I begin to resolve in my own mind, how I am to behave thro' life as a batchelor...

At this time he began a lifelong correspondence with Amelia Opie who was actually old enough to be his mother. His fears of remaining single were not realised; he actually married three times! Elizabeth describes in 1817 to her daughters Joseph John's marriage to Jane Birkbeck, (his first) as it took place in North Norfolk-

2 Bishop Ryder

The next morning we assembled the bride and bridegroom looking very sweet the bride with a rich light silk gown a white silk scarf white gloves black bonnet she look'd young lively and sweet, Joseph the grave friend but handsome and lovely. All the rest variously decorated in their best attire all appeared cheerful, easy, & comfortable though feeling the prospect a serious one. The carriages drove from the inn with our nice party & at Wells we met several more Catherine, Priscilla, poor Uncle Joseph and Jane my Uncle much overcome which we felt a good deal. The meeting was nearly full and a deeply interesting one.......after this we rode to Runcton enjoyed the bright day walk'd in the garden &c &c in different parties. The bride sweet and happy The bridegroom the same....the seaside beautiful I thought much of you my lov'd girls as I enjoyed my walks on the rocks with the bride and bridegroom....All the poor of the village had a treat of cake &c &c the farmers and gentry were all to be remember'd – we had a sweet serious time before we parted when we most of us went different ways the bride and bridegroom to a little country inn about 7 miles off in their way to Earlham where they meant to lodge.........

Eddington's edited Gurney manuscript

It is erroneously believed by those outside the Society that Elizabeth Fry is buried in the Gildencroft. She is, in fact, buried with her husband's family in Essex. Joseph John, banker, philanthropist, traveller on behalf of the Society of Friends at home and abroad, writer and leader of the Bible Society, was the last Gurney interment in 1847.

The local press was fulsome in its admiration in their obituary:

The decease of one who occupied so large a space in the estimation of his fellow citizens, and whose good deeds have 'fallen like the dew of heaven' upon all who have sought succour at his bounteous hand, must form an epoch in the history of the city of his birth, and in the present instance it is of no slight import to the religious and charitable society of which he was at once the ornament and the pride. Wherever good deeds were to be done, there was Mr Gurney's benevolent stretched out arm ready to comfort and aid those who were afflicted in mind, body or estate; and we in no degree exceed the bare limits of truth when we affirm that to the late Mr J. J. Gurney there is scarce an individual of the working classes, and many of the better orders in Norwich, who have not been in some degree succoured[sic] through his capacious and inexhaustible bounty. To every institution and charity in the city he was a liberal subscriber....

Norwich Mercury 1847

Anna Backhouse, J.J.'s daughter of his first marriage, wrote of her father

His word was law. It never entered our minds to disobey him... We were very little children when he began to take us into his study for times of religious retirement and prayer... the almost awful feeling of these occasions... he frequently impressed upon our minds the immediate and perceptible guidance of the Holy Spirit... the golden clue as he called it.

It was his custom in early life to rise betimes, and in order that he might secure alike his servant's punctuality as well as his own dispatch, he used when a young man to leave a sum in a certain spot with these orders, that if he was not dressed and in his study within a given time after being called, the money was to be taken for charitable purpose.

Mr Gurney was naturally gifted. He was tall and comely in person, with exceedingly handsome features, capable of great expression. In addressing is audience his manner was sedate and impressive and he was always listened to with a degree of respect which we scarcely remember to have been enjoyed by any other citizen.

Norwich Mercury 1847.

The Norwich Newspapers published obituaries in a similar vein for other members of the family upon their deaths. We offer further extracts:

Joseph Gurney. [d.1830]

Mr Gurney, in disposition, benevolence of intention, and purity of manners, approached as nearly the perfection of character sought by the Society of Friends as it is probably permitted to any human being to attain. The last years of his life were adorned by the useful, grave, and quiet studies which are now understood to dignify the intellectual hours of the Friends, but the business of his existence was to do good. In every endeavour to benefit or relieve the poor and needy he was amongst the foremost in purse and person. It is then in no strain of exaggeration that we describe his loss as a public misfortune, nor can we make more just record of his worth than to say that all who have borne or still bear the name of Gurney there is no one who has ennobled it more by active virtue....".

Norwich Mercury 1830

Hudson Gurney [d.1864]

Was a brilliant young man who did not enjoy banking at all, resigning his partnership in 1832. His tutors were both Quakers, John Hodgkin the calligrapher and 'Phenomenon' Young, doctor, physicist and master of 14 languages. At his home in St James Square, London he kept a library of 15,000 books, all of which he claimed to have read. His diaries were written in Greek so that his servants should not be able to understand themand he became a fellow of the Royal Society and Vice President of the Society of Antiquities.

Hudson developed a great love for and skill in writing poetry, writing advice to his banking friends and relatives in verse- On a box of bad bonds he put 'Wherein the Friends with might and main Both dunned and sued, but all in vain To get their money back again.....'

The Gurney Times Pamphlet issued by Barclays Bank to celebrate their Anniversary.

From Keswick to Intwood the road was a sea of human faces. The scholar was there to look his last upon a brother scholar; the gentleman of refined manners and delicate taste came to say goodbye to a departed gentleman; the struggling man whose struggles had been eased; the fallen man whose fortunes had been raised; the starving man whose belly had been filled; the diseased man whose disease had been charmed away by the coin of the departed; men, women and children were to be seen in throngs along the roads and abut the quaint old churchtard and all there to pay a last tribute to the lifelong goodness of Mr Hudson Gurney and he a millionaire from early life without a soul who envied him his wealth.

The procession left Keswick at about twenty minutes past eleven and consisted of twelve mourning coaches and seventeen private carriages and passed with its melancholy freight over a perfect carpet of leaves which as the wind lifted and whirled them in the air gave a mournful idea of the mutability of man.....

Norwich Mercury

Of all the members of the Gurney family, my favourite might be the feisty Henrietta (d. 1828). One of the six daughters of Henry Gurney, she never married, she remained the eternal maiden aunt, and could be relied on to pass opinion upon most things. Hannah Gurney describes the pattern of cousin Henrietta's visits to Earlham:

She also used to come in a very stiff stately dress and sit in great formality on the sofa. She also always brought her little box of sugar plums...

Henrietta habitually refused to pay her church tithes for the parish of St Michael at Plea in which she lived. There is, tucked away on a small sheet of yellowing paper in the archive a record of distraint completed a week or so after her death in 1828. Goods – six silver teaspoons and five other teaspoons to the value of £2:3/- plus 13/- costs- were taken and excluded from her estate for probate.

She also left a bequest in her will:

I give the sum of £100 to Norwich Monthly Meeting of the people called Quakers to be invested in the hands of Trustees for the benefit of its poor members...

Many small amounts were distributed to those in need, with several cheques forwarded to The Retreat in York until the residue was incorporated in the Meeting's Consolidated Charities, however the account book for this trust was badly water damaged in the Library Fire of 1994. It is a small soft notebook, covered at some point in parchment with the endpapers neatened with maroon marbled paper and faded fine hand lettering on the front. It was never considered important enough to be sent away with others for conservation. It still feels not damp; but certainly not dry and crisp, some of the page corners are stuck together and it retains a faint scent of burnt ash.

Friends were having difficulty paying the bills in the late 1820s for the new Meeting House at Goat Lane and massively overdrawn on its budget. Henrietta she wrote not long before her death in 1828 to the Convenor of the Committee (which was entirely male) who, having commissioned the building's construction, was now charged with solving the problems:

Vain as I may appear I cannot help saying there are certain things in which women are the best judges and I believe that had we been more consulted some errors would have been prevented and greater convenience ensured. Excuse this from thy vain Friend...

There are 56 graves in the Gildencroft of those still with the surname Gurney and any number of others related, Aggs, Hoares, Birkbecks, Ketts; daughters, cousins and sisters who have married other bankers and husbands of that class.

JOHN PARKER. DIED 9TH November 1727[3]

How would you feel if the one thing your Ffriends could say about you after your death is that you kept your Ministry short "fearful of Running into too many words… lest [you] should Runn into Disorder and Confusion"?

Our Ffriend John Parker was Born of parents who not only made a profession of Christian Religion as it is held forth by our Ffriends as a people, but were also Concerned to Educate him in ye principles and way of truth, wherein both his father and mother were good Examples to him.

In his very Young Years he was Remarkably Sober and not given to so much Idleness and vanity as many Young Men delight themselves in: and we have Reason to believe that he applied himself Early to seeking after ye knowledge of God and ye way of Life and salvation.

About the Age of twenty six years he forst appeared in Publick Testimony, speaking sometimes a few words in our Meeting to the satisfaction of Friends in general and we believe to ye Edification of some in particular, his Ministry being plain and Instructive and Erdently springing from the Grace of god, whereby his heart was kept in an humble frame before ye Lord, whose servant he was Concerned to approve himself.

His testimonies for severall years after his Coming forth in ye Ministry were in common but short, for as it was his constant Care to Minister in ye Openings of ye spiritt of Life and purely of ye ability that God was pleased to give, so he was fearfull of Running into too many words, or endeavouring to appear in long Discourses least he should thereby loose ye sencible guidance and assistance of ye Holy Spiritt in ye Exercise of his Ministry and Runn into such Disorder and Confusion that would render his labours not only of no Service to those that heard him, but give reason of scandal to that holy Principle he made Profession of.

For severall years before his Death it pleased The Lord to enlarge his Gift to which further dispensation he was faithfull, Labouring According to his ability to promote ye honour of God and ye good and welfare of his Church and People...

…He was of but mean sircomstances in ye world and had a pretty large family of Children whom he Reputedly supported by his own care

3 See chapter headed Gravemakers and Headstones where Parker is asked to negotiate with The Widow Byar.

and Industry and when he found himself Concerned to go any Journey in ye service of truth would take uncommon pains to Acquire by his labour a sufficiency for ye support of his wife and family in his Absence, he was generally very expeditious in his travels, being for pressing forward as he found himself clear of any Meeting he visited.

His Conversation was serious and Commendable and his deportment in Life was such as gained him much esteem a mong many people who were not of our Profession, and we think we may further say of him that he was a Man of Uprightness and Integrity, one that truly loved and feared ye Lord and that was Concerned to serve him faithfully in his Age and Generation.

He was brought Low by his bodily Infirmities for sometime before his end, yet was no weak as to be wholly confined to his house, but walked about his business to ye day of his departure, which was on ye 9th day of ye 11th mo. Last and on ye 12th day of ye same month was buried in Friends Burial Ground in this City.

N.R.O. SF64

The problem, for me, is this 'Testimony To The Grace Of God As Shown In The Life Of' is not an obituary, hardly a proper biography of the man. It doesn't say, for example, how he acquired "by his labour a sufficiency to support his family", nor how he came to be in "mean sircomstances".

His short pieces of vocal Ministry, "Openings of ye Spiritt of Life", suggest that he may have spoken the Truth in Love: Good Honest Quaker Directness. We can all say we have known some of that! Compare Parker's testimony with the testimony for William Forster which goes on for more than ten pages in a huge ledger portraying more of a Saint (with perhaps a few frailties) than a Human Being. Look closely though, the clues are there: Stubborness: always right when others suggest he is wrong. The testimony for Joseph Gurney in 1746 tells us that for the last eighteen years of his life

it pleased the Almighty in the Course of his Providence to permit this our dear Friend to be tryed with… the Stone and Gravil… hardly in that time enjoying one Day of Perfect health….

Bladder stones though? Possibly too much information both for him and his family and for us.

Epilogue

We set out on this journey through the Gildencroft Burial Ground with the fervent hope that others would become interested in those Quakers who had lived before us and that we might learn a little from their lives. We were also conscious that our present Trustees had been faced with a crumbling wall around the ground and had, in good stewardship, taken the difficult decision to use some of our capital reserves to carry out the repairs. We hope that any profit from this volume may help to offset some of that cost.

However, those that took that difficult decision may feel comforted that things (historically at least) don't change. In 1756, less than a hundred years after it was constructed, the same wall was crumbling...

> *The Friends appointed to inspect into the state of the wall of the Burial ground report that having themselves examined the same, and also had the Assistance of Workmen, are of the Opinion that to repair it, the Cost will near equal the rebuilding: and as it may yet safely continue for some time, this Meeting defers doing anything thereto until it shall become more absolutely needful...*

So they left it. Now we in the twentyfirst century have to pick up the pieces... Literally.

Friends, things are now ABSOLUTELY MORE NEEDFUL.